TEACHING TECHNIQUES
IN ADULT EDUCATION

Teaching Techniques
in Adult Education

Edited by

MICHAEL D. STEPHENS, MA, MEd, PhD

Assistant Director and Head of the Division
of Adult Education

and

GORDON W. RODERICK, BSc, PhD, AInstP

Senior Assistant Director and Head of
the Special Courses Division

The Institute of Extension Studies, University of Liverpool

DAVID & CHARLES
NEWTON ABBOT   LONDON   VANCOUVER

0 7153 5205 9

© David & Charles and contributors 1971, 1974

Library of Congress Catalog Card No 74-15794

Printed in Great Britain
by Redwood Burn Ltd Trowbridge & Esher
for David & Charles (Holdings) Limited
South Devon House Newton Abbot Devon

Published in Canada by Douglas David & Charles Limited
3645 McKechnie Drive West Vancouver BC

Contents

Foreword

By Thomas Kelly

The character and concept of adult education in Britain have changed radically even within the lifetime of many of its present practitioners. At the outbreak of World War II the term 'adult education' was very much a term of art, restricted in common usage to courses of liberal study provided by the 'responsible bodies' ie by the university extra-mural departments and a group of voluntary organisations of which the most important was the Workers' Educational Association. It was these bodies—first the universities, then the WEA, then the two together —which had been the pioneers in provision for the non-vocational education of adults, and they still dominated the field. The local education authorities had, it is true, their evening institutes, but half the students were under eighteen, taking either continuation classes or low-level vocational classes in such subjects as shorthand and typing; the classes in cookery, dressmaking, handicrafts and the like which constituted the main provision for older people were not really thought of as adult education. Only a few LEAs, notably the London County Council, had centres specially devoted to the non-vocational education of adults.

Since the war the composition of the responsible bodies has changed somewhat—there are now more university responsible bodies and fewer non-university ones—but their work has continued to increase. By 1966 they were providing in England and Wales more than three times as many grant-aided courses as in 1938, with four times as many enrolled students. These raw figures, however, do not indicate the change in the character of the work.

The university extra-mural departments, for their part, have become increasingly involved in training and refresher courses, especially for teachers and for the growing army of social workers; and this tendency has been reinforced by the advent of the new universities, many of which have brought with them from a former existence a well-established tradition of technological refresher courses. More and more university adult education is thus being directed to professional ends, and the old

7

tradition of learning for learning's sake, though it continues to flourish, seems in danger of being overshadowed.

The WEA, meanwhile, has maintained the tradition of liberal adult education, though in its ordinary classes it has to a large extent lost contact with the 'labouring classes' it was created to serve. In compensation, however, it has since the war been making determined and successful efforts (often in collaboration with extra-mural departments) to cater for the needs of the workers through day-release courses, factory-based courses, and pre-retirement courses, and more recently through work in the educational priority areas. These developments have been helped by the disappearance in 1965 of the WEA's former Marxist rival, the National Council of Labour Colleges.

The most important change, however, has been the emergence of the local education authorities as major providers. The transformation of the old-style evening institute into the new-style adult education centre, providing such subjects as painting, sculpture, pottery, music, films, photography, local history, languages, and a wide range of recreational subjects, has indeed been spectacular, and is all the more remarkable in that it has been achieved with such very modest resources. The public response, too, has been magnificent, and in spite of setbacks caused by repeated economy campaigns the number of adult students in the evening institutes of England and Wales had by 1967 reached 1,100,000, compared with 240,000 in the courses run by responsible bodies. These figures exclude enrolments in the thirty or so short-term residential colleges, nearly all post-war creations and most of them under LEA auspices.

All this has led people to take a much larger view of what constitutes adult education. Instead of being a rather esoteric hobby of an academically minded minority, it is more and more coming to embrace, as the words would themselves suggest, all forms of education for adults, including recreational education and in some degree vocational education as well. The establishment after the war of the National Institute of Adult Education has done much to foster this new attitude by bringing together for consultative purposes not only representatives of the LEAs and the responsible bodies, but also representatives of bodies engaged in adult education of a much less formal kind, eg the Women's Institutes and the Townswomen's Guilds.

By the bibliographies and inquiries it has published, the National Institute has also done much to stimulate the study of adult education itself: its history and organisation; the characteristics and motives of its students; the processes of adult learning; and the various techniques of teaching. There are still those who look back nostalgically to the days when inspiration and a modicum of knowledge were sufficient qualifications for any teacher of adults, but inspired teachers are few, the demand is constantly growing, and if adult education is to attain its true importance in society we must be prepared to train people to the same level of professional competence as we would expect in other branches of the education service. Many university extra-mural departments have already begun to do this, and a considerable range of full-time and part-time diploma and certificate courses in adult education is now available, eg in Edinburgh, Glasgow, Hull, Liverpool, Manchester and Nottingham.

These courses in turn have led to a further widening of the field, because as soon as one begins to analyse adult education for training purposes one realises that there are certain basic problems, for example in adult learning and in teaching methods, which are common to all forms of adult education, and that from the methodological point of view the sharp distinction formerly drawn between vocational and non-vocational adult education is quite irrelevant. Lessons derived from industrial training may be of vital significance in the craft classes of the evening institute, and a study of the nature and value of discussion in the tutorial class may throw important light on the problems of the teacher in a technical college.

The training courses have also revealed that there are all kinds of people outside the field of adult education who find the skills of the adult educator of value in their jobs. The applicants for courses thus include not only those engaged in adult education for the responsible bodies and the LEAs, but also technical college lecturers, lecturers in colleges of education, personnel officers, management consultants, trade union officials, co-operative workers, doctors, nurses, youth workers and a great variety of social and community workers.

A process of interpenetration is thus developing over the whole field of adult education and allied activities, to the great benefit of all concerned. There has been much useful exchange of experience and much experiment in new teaching techniques. This wider and more liberal outlook is reflected in the chapters that follow, which will, I believe, be of value to adult education practitioners in many different fields.

1 Introduction:
The Teaching of Adults

Michael D. Stephens and Gordon W. Roderick

THE RANGE OF ADULT CLASSES

The variety of provision within the field of adult education in England and Wales is considerable. The local education authorities furnish classes through evening institutes, colleges of further education and technical colleges, colleges of art, polytechnics and commercial colleges. Other major contributions come from the responsible bodies (mainly university extra-mural departments and the Workers' Educational Association) which provide a range of courses, some vocationally orientated, for instance training courses for social workers, others mainly non-vocational in purpose, on topics such as local history and philosophy. There are short-term and long-term residential colleges. Some adults are involved in schemes to prepare them for university or college of education places. Courses are also available to adult students partly or entirely through television or radio.[1] A substantial demand is met by correspondence programmes.[2] Numerous other bodies, such as the National Union of Townswomen's Guilds and the YMCA, also offer courses in fields of adult education.

The extensive range of adult classes covers innumerable educational opportunities such as studying for a university degree or learning the skills of dressmaking. It is important to emphasise this variety; yet we believe that despite such a diversity of classes the fact that the teacher in each situation is dealing with adult students provides a strong enough common link to justify a general text on teaching techniques in adult education.

ADULT STUDENTS

The adult student's expectations of the teacher will be at least partly coloured by his school experience. At school he probably expected many

11

teachers to be indifferent, or possibly even incompetent in their abilities. The good one was received gratefully by the pupils. Therefore adult students often come to classes anticipating poor, slovenly or superficial teaching. If their expectations are confirmed they may leave in a state of dangerous disappointment, permanently convinced that education remains a field of second-raters.

Nevertheless there are differences between the adult student and the school pupil. He will no longer accept imposed discipline as a child will. Despite the remarkable politeness of the adult student, he is more likely to become vocal if the depths of a poor teaching situation are plumbed. Adults have been known to take their protests to the extent of striking when their injustices have not been dealt with.

The adult student's reasons for attending a class will also be more varied than the child's, who is bound by law to go to school. In a survey we carried out amongst women attending evening institute dressmaking classes on Merseyside we found some came to learn about the subject, while many others wanted to have a night out or make new friends. Some liked working with a particular teacher, while others came in the hope that the acquisition of the skill would aid the family budget. We were most impressed by the diversity of reasons, from one woman who saw her class as a training for her school teaching commitments to a number who were using such pursuits as an escape from the boredom of their role as housewives. Most of the 277 women we asked were motivated by more than one factor. Also, within the reasons given, there were differences of emphasis; for example, some wished to feel part of a group whilst others wanted to gain some form of recognition by the other group members.

THE TEACHER OF ADULTS

The aim of this volume is to discuss techniques which will help to make teachers of adults more effective. Although there are individuals who are born teachers, these are comparative rarities, and of greater interest is the average teacher who can improve on his success with his adult classes by study and experiment.

What are some of the characteristics of a good teacher of adults?[3] Because each teacher is unique any definition inevitably represents a generalisation; he will like people, and act intelligently towards them; despite his own intelligence he will not be contemptuous towards students who are of limited ability; he will be good humoured; he will view every class as a group of very varied personalities who need the maximum aid he can give, mainly in educational terms, but also sometimes in social terms; he will be tactful and fair, energetic and articulate, imaginative and adaptable.

The teacher must know his subject thoroughly, and present information in a way which is not heavy or wooden. Sarcasm or bullying in an adult class will produce protest or withdrawal. It is very easy to be superficial as a teacher, and this emphasises the need for good preparation and the fact that effective tuition involves much hard work.

Adult students can be divided into those who want to learn and those who must be persuaded to learn. The former will learn with any but the most ineffectual of teachers, while the latter need inducements such as, for example, advancement in their jobs. However, it is important to stress the differences between teaching adults and teaching children. The most obvious of these is the maturity of the adult. This factor alone makes the teaching of adults most rewarding. With adults it is easier to ascertain the extent to which they have been helped towards their goals, and this is true whether these are vocational or non-vocational. Such knowledge acts as an incomparable recompense to the teacher for all his efforts during the course.

The Role of the Teacher

In adult education the role of the teacher is to help the students fulfil themselves as human beings. The teacher must, therefore, not only be an expert in his subject or skill, but also have imagination and compassion and the ability to communicate his knowledge.

Most students will expect the teacher first and foremost to provide and interpret information relevant to their particular field of study. In this the teacher's role is that of encouraging the student to greater independence of thought and work, allied to higher standards of performance. The teacher must ensure that the student makes consistent progress in mastering the skill or subject under study.

Particularly in non-vocational adult education, the role of the teacher will be allied to the class function as a social focus. The teacher should endeavour to maximise the contribution that the social contacts within the class situation provide for each student. He will thus help in transforming a number of individuals into a group. Within this situation the teacher may find himself in the role of a counsellor. However, the good teacher will ensure that the social function of the class is an aid to the group's educational progress. A 'tea-and-gossip' course should not come within the field of responsibility of an educational budget.

The teacher also has a role as a 'liberalising' factor in the lives of his students. Professor Jones, in the final chapter of this volume, defines the term 'liberal' with admirable clarity. Education, and particularly adult education, must inevitably be based on a set of values. Many teachers find this the hardest part to fulfil effectively. Despite such considerations, the role of the adult teacher is only partly served if he fails to widen the vision of his students and improve their judgement.

In addition the teacher must take full advantage of the opportunities provided by the student's desire to learn. This implies a great deal more than just instruction in the subject or skill. Besides a target of excellence in the subject studied in adult classes, most teachers find themselves involved in questions of judgement and value. Such social factors as the complexities of human relationships within a group will be of importance.[4] In the area of liberal studies a teacher of motor maintenance, besides instructing students in the technicalities of their cars, may find himself involved in discussions on planned obsolescence, the breathalyser or the responsibilities of the mechanic in a garage checking vehicle brakes. These questions from the class, and the discussion they engender, may well lead on to broader issues related to the society of which the students are a part. The teacher of motor maintenance could find his class trying to define their attitudes on beauty or truth or goodness after discussing their cars as symbols of modern society.

Another important question the teacher must ask himself is whether the work is of continual challenge to the students. This raises the problem of recognising when some of the students have passed from challenge to bafflement. The role of the teacher demands sensitivity, but even one who is sensitive to the teaching situation may not be able to discover, with some of his students, when he has reached this point. In practical subjects bafflement tends to show itself more easily by a student's inability to continue a project, but in other subjects the teacher may need to carry out frequent tests to find whether the lesson pace has been too fast or too slow. In a language class a teacher can test orally the progress of the students. A teacher of philosophy can question students on difficult points, periodically give out short questionnaire tests, and also ask for essays. These are some suggestions, but an obvious point to be made is that if any student looks baffled the teacher must stop immediately and determine what his problem is. If it is a problem for one student, in all probability others will be facing similar difficulties.

Teaching Aims

The teacher of adults may find that his teaching aims differ from the aims and expectations of his students. As in all teaching situations involving adults, the teacher must retain a flexibility of approach in order to get the most from his syllabus. Before formulating the teaching aims of a course it is advisable, if at all possible, to discuss the programme with the students.

The course must make the best use of the student's time. This will entail the teacher asking questions of himself and of the students throughout the programme. Are some students neglected? Is there adequate student activity? Is there enough reference to work which could be done outside the limited class time (eg book lists, projects etc)?[5] Are the students' interests and capabilities familiar to the teacher? Is enough time being devoted to discussing the broader issues involved in the programme? Is the best use made of audio-visual aids?[6] Is the working environment satisfactory or could it be improved? Do the students know how to take notes effectively?[7] Does the teacher keep a record of each student's progress? Such records need not be elaborate, but might well include a regular assessment of the student's work by the teacher (eg in a dressmaking class the teacher should ensure that the progress of each student's work is noted each week), and a marking down of absences so that allowances can be made for missed lessons. The teacher must see that he allows time at each meeting for students to bring up difficulties that occur (a record of these should be kept). Inevitably he will find that he needs to design his own records.

Very few adults coming to a class will have a clear-cut idea of how they should be taught, but they offer a maturity which involves strongly-held views on many issues, both major and minor. In the teaching aims there will be a need for compromise between the teacher and the student. Both the teacher and the adult student should find such class contact a rewarding educational process. Although motives, views and expectations will differ from student to student and from class to class, there will be a need to find something of a middle course between these and what the teacher considers to be the academic requirements and aims of the programme. Within the framework of an adult class there will be ample scope for trying various teaching techniques in an effort to achieve a satisfactory programme from the viewpoint of both the teacher and the student.

Teaching Methods

The selection of a suitable method of tuition demands that the teacher should answer a number of questions. What is expected from the class by both the teacher and the students? Who are the students? How best can the themes of the class be put over? No doubt each teacher will have many other questions which come to mind in the planning stage of a programme. To decide upon a particular method without attempting to answer such questions will make the task of the teacher considerably harder and the result less satisfactory.

It is not realistic to suggest any hard and fast rules regarding the selection of teaching methods. It is hoped that the following chapters will provide the teacher with a wide range of techniques to permit him to choose for himself. Every method has advantages and limitations, and in any teaching situation the environment and resources will dictate the techniques which can be used.

THE TEACHING ENVIRONMENT

The Physical Environment

Often effective teaching is held back because of purely physical factors. It is important to ensure that the students are warm enough, that the ventilation of the classroom is adequate etc. Although there is often no alternative to such accommodation problems as arise in the teaching of adult students in the classrooms of primary schools, it is always possible to make sure that the very best in terms of physical comfort is made of the situation.

A businesslike attitude towards the possible difficulties of the classroom is the best way to get the students working. It is not a matter of just caring for the students' comfort, but a question of preparing them for work. The hesitant and inefficient teacher distracts the student, as also does discomfort. Some teachers are able to create an appropriate atmosphere to encourage the work of the students in classrooms which would be the despair of less effective colleagues.

The teacher must help his students by providing as good a working area as the resources will permit. The classroom must be checked by the teacher before it is used. If chairs are moved within the room they should be put back afterwards so that smooth relations with other important members of staff such as caretakers may be ensured. The pottery class without enough kiln firing-time for its work, or a centre without storage space for the woodwork class, may provide insurmountable problems, but such a conclusion should be reached only after all the possibilities for improvement have been explored.

The Social Environment

A majority of adult students have a wish for social contact within the class. In this the teacher can act as a catalyst in order that the class members may get to know each other. Good relations between class members will go a long way towards producing a good working environment in which education can take place.

Not only must there be student involvement within the group, but also teacher involvement with the students. The teacher who systematically gets to know his students will provide them with the satisfaction of feeling that they are cared for as individuals, and the teacher who knows what to ask his students to give to the group will have progressed far in meeting the demands of the social situation within which he and his students work. As student social needs have to be served within the class, it is preferable to aim at processes of group learning rather than a two-way relationship between teacher and individual.[8]

With increasing success in the matter of the social environment of the class the group may well need expression of its existence as an entity. This can usually be achieved by shared tea-breaks or class parties or outings. In this catering for members' social needs it is vital that the dominant consideration of enlightened educational development be not lost. It is very easy for a class to become exclusive and stagnate. The teacher must emphasise that the group is part of a larger organisation. Both socially and educationally it will benefit the class members if there is contact with other classes. Unfortunately, students from different groups do not mix without the deliberate action of the teachers or the administrative staff of the institution concerned. Such joint ventures as projects or exhibitions or instruction given by team teaching[9] can provide an environment in which students from different classes get to know each other.

Satisfaction will be derived by the students if they are given a feeling of responsibility for the work carried out within the institution. A belief that they are members of an institution and not just members of a class will aid morale and also bring advantages to the institution itself. The concept of 'we' rather than 'them and us' will serve both the social and educational needs of the students while making the institution a more efficient unit.

An institution which aims at making all its students feel themselves to be part of it must see that they are fully informed of all developments within the institution's programme. Along with this there must be ample opportunity for the students to be able to develop new interests. Also important is continuity, and a well-formulated legislative framework can provide a good foundation for such continuity, so that there is a firm membership basis, a constitution, and financial arrangements which help in establishing a tradition of student participation.

To give students within an institution responsibilities often proves the most successful way of achieving a feeling of personal commitment and sense of belonging. Because of the numbers involved, permitting all students to vote on every issue that arises is usually too cumbersome. In most instances the students should elect a council from among themselves to act on their behalf. Such a student council must then be given responsibilities worthy of adults. The council's position within the institution's framework must be clearly stated within the constitution.

B

A students' council which functions as a mere social committee will be of little use in promoting the overall efficiency of an adult institution. Responsibilities such as a say in the spending of the institution's money should be aimed at.

The quality and variety of the institution's teaching programme will benefit greatly by having the student council's advice during its formulation. Not only will the students gain both socially and educationally, but a programme to which they have contributed in the planning stage will also demand that they share the responsibility of making it a success. An institution is part of a community. The social life of the community is important to the institution, which should serve its area both within its walls and outside. Adults can be made more aware of the needs of their community.

The aim of an adult institution must be to enrich the quality of the life lived both within the institution and within the society of which it is a part. Teachers and principals should be given time to reflect on their work in order to decide how most effectively to achieve this aim. Adult institutions should not only be places of involvement, but should also contribute to the creativity of a community. The class activities should lead to new organisations within the institution's area. Because of its educational resources an adult institution is well placed to carry out research into the needs, pattern and trends of the community of which it is a part. It can make the community more aware of its own potentialities.

EVALUATION[10]

The function of evaluation is to find out to what extent the aims and objectives of a teacher's course have been achieved. This means evaluating both the teacher's teaching and the student's learning. Evaluation is something that every teacher should practise all the time, if only in the form of asking 'have they got that?' There is always a danger of viewing it as an extra ingredient in the teacher's mix instead of a vital part. As Bergevin and McKinley[11] state, 'Without periodic evaluation, goals are lost sight of, programs tend to fall into purposeless, unchanging patterns, inappropriate methods become habitual, and progress is not pointed out and cannot serve as an incentive'.

However, it must be stressed that evaluation is not without its difficulties. Programme objectives are often unstated or vague or in dispute (this is particularly true in non-vocational adult education). Students have a complexity which makes measurement difficult. Measuring educational change also offers problems. The variety of the constituent parts of the educational pattern makes interpretation difficult, but evaluation remains the only effective way of course assessment.

There are different levels of evaluation. The adult educator may wish to look at the provision over a country as a whole or within a single institution, or to assess a course or a part of a course. Despite these different levels there are certain fundamental characteristics. Specific measurable objectives for a course must be set. It must be decided what evidence will be accepted as indicating that the objectives have been gained; when this evidence is available it must be collected and the results analysed. After such analysis conclusions may be drawn. From this it becomes obvious that evaluation must be one of the first considerations when planning a course. As a mere appendage to a course it will provide unacceptable and unsatisfactory results.

There are three obvious factors which will influence the whole question of programme evaluation. The greater the complexity of the objectives the more challenging will be the problem of evaluation. Also of significance is the length of the course. Evaluation may well prove much easier on a one-year residential programme than on a ten-meeting non-residential course. In the former there will be much more time for both measurement and the development of evidence of objectives attained. Finally, it is somewhat easier to evaluate a formal educational programme than an informal one, where it is more difficult to measure the fluid situation and the students are more likely to resent evaluation as an intrusion.

One of the most difficult parts of evaluation comes at the beginning of a programme with the need to establish clear objectives. Although this demands precision on the part of the course planners, unless such objectives are defined and accepted evaluation may well prove a worthless exercise. In determining the objectives it is a considerable advantage if those enrolling can give their reasons for coming. The objectives must be practical ones (ie within the scope of programme achievement) with which the teacher feels himself in sympathy. They must provide a foundation for further development, and must be acceptable to the students.

Evidence with regard to the success of a programme in moving towards its objectives may be collected in a variety of ways; usually a combination of a number of these will need to be employed. The student can be given a carefully prepared questionnaire or periodic tests. There is a tradition of assessing students on the basis of written work submitted regularly to the teacher. Although there is always the problem of programme disruption, an interviewer can be used or the class can be observed. If the resources are available class behaviour can be recorded on tape or by camera for later assessment. The major problem in the collecting of such evidence is to ensure its validity. The technique employed must be well suited to the educational situation involved, but there is always the difficulty that the moment any such technique is used a new and artificial situation may well be created. Students may find difficulty in forgetting the presence of a camera or an observer and act in an unnatural fashion. Such problems demand the full participation of all those involved in the course (teachers, students, administrators etc), and the collection of evidence in the maximum number of ways which will not disrupt the course and for which adequate resources and time are available.

In most instances the easiest evidence to handle is that which can be counted, but much will be in the form of description, which is more difficult to categorise. After the analysis of the evidence which has been collected, an assessment in relation to course aims may lead to the modification of the course involving new objectives or a change of content to achieve the original objectives more effectively. There will be a need to view critically the evaluation at all stages to avoid taking programme decisions on the basis of poor or inadequate assessment.

Of course, every evaluation is to a greater or lesser extent a generalisation. Each teaching situation is a unique occasion which will emphasise this fact. No teacher gives an identical second period, nor does any student act precisely the same way in any two lessons. Such variety and such danger of generalisation makes it important to ensure that any evaluation models employed are used sensitively.

Measurement

Verner and Booth[12] list four major areas where 'educational goals . . . can be evaluated with some confidence'. These are knowledge or information measurement, attitude measurement, skill measurement, and acceptance and adoption measurement. The tests available regarding content are numerous, but the teacher may prefer to construct his own. Similarly, advice on attitude measurement is readily available from any university department of psychology or sociology, whether the interest is in specific or general attitude modification. In skill measurement each part of the operation must be isolated and observed independently. The acceptance and adoption of ideas or practices measurement are comparatively new, but much has been written about it.[13]

In measuring changes which take place during the course, the first need is to identify factors which show change, eg by written tests or by verbal questioning or by the observation of the performance of a skill. Having noted such changes, it must then be decided how they are to be measured, ie whether the student is to be tested or whether the teacher is to observe or if a third party is to be brought in to evaluate.

Each measuring tool must have certain characteristics. It must measure precisely and clearly, supply comparable information from all individuals and situations being measured, and should not, if possible, be over elaborate. If the teacher has doubts about the construction of such a tool in his course evaluation, the advice of an expert should be sought.

Finally, it is perhaps useful to illustrate such tools with a well known form of scale for testing attitude: [14]

The following list consists of statements about China.[18] After reading each statement, please indicate your agreement or disagreement with it in terms of the key which follows. This is not a test of 'right' and 'wrong' answers, but of your reaction.

Key: A = I strongly agree or accept the statement.
B = I tend to agree or accept the statement.
C = I am uncertain or have no opinion.
D = I tend to disagree or reject the statement.
E = I strongly disagree or reject the statement.

A. B. C. D. E. 1 China is a very aggressive state.
A. B. C. D. E. 2 China is motivated by nationalism, not communism.
A. B. C. D. E. 3 The world would be a safer place without China.
A. B. C. D. E. 4 China would be better without Mao Tse-tung.
A. B. C. D. E. 5 To understand China you need to understand her history.
A. B. C. D. E. 6 The only thing the Chinese do well is multiply themselves.
A. B. C. D. E. 7 China will use her nuclear weapons against the West when she is strong enough.
A. B. C. D. E. 8 It is in Britain's interest to persuade the Soviet Union to attack China.
A. B. C. D. E. 9 China has no tradition of civilisation to give her stability.
A. B. C. D. E. 10 The West should attack China before she becomes too strong.
A. B. C. D. E. 11 Population problems will always stop China becoming a developed country.
A. B. C. D. E. 12 China has caused the Vietnam War.
A. B. C. D. E. 13 China has no right to a place in the United Nations assembly.
A. B. C. D. E. 14 China will cause a Third World War.

The variations which can be put together regarding such a questionnaire are legion, and it is up to the teacher to shape such tools to his course-evaluation needs. Whether it is evaluation by examinations, marked essays, pieces of work, notes in the teacher's record book or some other means the teacher will need to tailor the method so that it '. . . provides the means to assess the effectiveness of instruction, to compare the efficiency of processes, and to analyse the suitability of content'.[16] Only through continuous evaluation of both the teacher's teaching and the student's learning can knowledge of effectiveness be established.

CONCLUSION

To summarise what has been discussed in this chapter it is suggested that the foremost need in the teaching of adults is sensitivity. The teacher must be responsive to the demands of the teaching situation in which he finds himself. Such sensitivity can be illustrated by the importance the teacher gives to matters like evaluation. A teacher who fails to treat evaluation as an integral and vital part of the course on which he is teaching is unlikely to be fully responsive to other aspects of the teacher's work and role.

Of great importance, too, is flexibility. Effective teachers are rarely disconcerted by the failure of the perfect physical or intellectual environment to materialise. With determination and enthusiasm almost any problem likely to arise in the teaching of adults can be solved.

Finally, much of what has been said can be summed up in a quotation from the writings of Hutchinson[17]:

> . . . Teaching methods and techniques must take into account:
> expressed and implied demands;
> the character and strength of motivation in
> relation to varying degrees of individual capacity;
> the extent and nature of previous education;
> the practical possibilities of time and place.

NOTES

1 See Ch 13
2 See Ch 14
3 See also Chs 3 and 11
4 This is dealt with more fully in Ch 3
5 See Ch 9
6 See Ch 10
7 See Ch 9
8 See Ch 3
9 Team Teaching. This is where two or more teachers have the responsibility for the total tuition of a group on a course. It covers a wide variety of organisational patterns, ranging from lectures to large groups to individual study. Team members plan, carry out and evaluate the work undertaken by the students and staff. Joint planning and evaluation are an integral part of team teaching
10 See also Ch 12
11 Bergevin, P. and McKinley, J. *Design for Adult Education in the Church* (Connecticut 1961), 94
12 Much of this section is based on Verner, C. and Booth, A. *Adult Education* (Washington 1964)
13 Rogers, E. M. *Diffusion of Innovations* (New York 1962)

14   Miller, H. L. *Teaching and Learning in Adult Education* (1964) 329-31
15   The authors have used variations of this short test at the beginning and conclusion of extra-mural courses on modern China
16   Verner, C. and Booth, A. *Adult Education,* 104
17   Hutchinson, E. M. 'Adult Education' in *Techniques of Teaching* vol 3 : *Tertiary Education,* Peterson, A.D.C.(ed), (Oxford 1965), 113

FURTHER READING

Bergevin, P. and McKinley, J. *Design for Adult Education in the Church* (Connecticut 1961)

Dees, N. (ed). *Approaches to Adult Teaching* (Oxford 1965)

Dressel, P. *Evaluation in Higher Education* (Boston 1961)

Miller, H. L. *Teaching and Learning in Adult Education* (1964)

Miller, H. L. and McGuire, C. H. *Evaluating Liberal Adult Education* (Chicago 1961)

Morgan, B., Holmes, G. E. and Bundy, C. E. *Methods of Adult Education* (Danville, Illinois 1960)

Peterson, A. D. C. (ed). *Techniques of Teaching,* vol 3 : *Tertiary Education* (Oxford 1965)

Robinson, J. and Barnes, N. (eds). *New Media and Methods in Industrial Training* (1968)

Rogers, E. M. *Diffusion of Innovations* (New York 1962)

Rogers, J. (ed). *Teaching on Equal Terms* (1969)

Solomon, D., Bezdek, W. E. and Rosenberg, L. *Teaching Styles and Learning* (Chicago 1963)

Verner, C. and Booth, A. *Adult Education* (Washington 1964)

Wientge, K. M. 'A Model for the Analysis of Continuing Education for Adults', *Adult Education* (US), 16 (Summer 1966)

2 Adult Learning

Linda Thompson

THE LEARNING PROCESS

L earning is invisible. It is a mysterious and unreliable process which cannot be directly observed or reliably controlled. The eminent neurologist Sir Charles Sherrington once said that, for all we knew about the workings of the brain, it might as well be made of cotton wool. Accepting these limitations, it is still possible to construct a model of the processes involved in learning. The mind or brain of the learner may be visualised as a closed black box, whose contents and workings are inaccessible. Clues can be obtained from controlling, as far as possible, what 'goes in', examining what 'comes out' and thus deducing what went on in between.

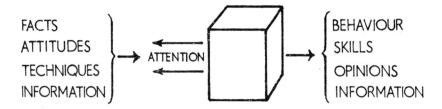

This diagram represents the black box with its input and output. The box itself contains impressions of the learner's previous experience, which will influence learning so that the output cannot be predicted from the input. It will be seen in addition that the factor of attention must be considered. Learning may then be defined as the process which changes the individual's way of responding as a result of environmental experience.

The Senses

The environment can only affect the learner by means of the senses and nervous system. Information must be available in a form which the senses can register, or it is lost. There are at least seven senses. The five most commonly known ones are those which simply receive information from 'out there'; the other two deal with location in the environment. The first five—vision, hearing, taste, touch and smell—are familiar, though more complex than this familiarity might suggest.

The two senses which provide information about position and movement in the environment are those of equilibrium and kinaesthesis. Equilibrium, or balance, is most easily demonstrated in learning to ride a bicycle. Kinaesthesis is the awareness of one's position in space and the relative location of the limbs; this may sound complex but can be demonstrated by the ability of most people, when sober, to close the eyes, extend the arms, and bring both forefingers to rest on the end of the nose. These two senses are used in any learning task which involves more than sitting to read or listen.

Imagery

Most learning tasks involve a number of senses; selection of the appropriate ones will be governed by individual differences as well as by the requirements of the task. Differing sensory preferences are reflected in the individual's imagery, which in most cases is predominantly visual or auditory. In recalling the number of days in a month, many people use the mnemonic rhyme 'thirty days hath September' and may 'hear' it either inwardly or aloud as they recite it. Others with a predominantly visual memory may imagine the rhyme written down or visualise a calendar. Children often have particularly acute visual imagery which may make it difficult to distinguish between reality and imagination. After reading a story about a tiger, for example, a child may believe he saw one in the garden, so vivid is the image in his mind. Later, this capacity may be useful in visualising pages of notes or text in an examination. Such imagery is called 'eidetic', but is better known to most people as a photographic memory. Eidetic imagery rarely persists beyond childhood but it is not known why this is so.

It is also possible to have a primarily kinaesthetic memory; for instance, trying to recall a manual task one may mime the sequence of events with one's hands in the same way that someone with an auditory memory may repeat the instructions for performing the task under his breath. These forms of imagery and memory are not mutually exclusive; most people can use all these methods, but in each individual one or other is likely to predominate. The implications of these individual differences for the teacher of adults will be discussed later in this chapter.

Selection

The senses, as well as being the means by which we make contact with the outside world, have an important role as filters. There is so much going on in the environment that the brain would be overwhelmed if it tried to register it all. Driving along a road, for example, one is bombarded with information from a number of sources—noises, sights, movements, and instruments on the dashboard. Without selection and the suppression of a large proportion of these stimuli one would be likely to miss such vital stimuli as a traffic light turning red or an unwary pedestrian stepping off the pavement. An important aspect of learning any complex skill such as driving is learning what to ignore.

Filtering takes place at a number of levels, most of which are pre-conscious. At the simplest visual level, the eye 'often instructs rather than informs the brain by sorting out its messages in advance, discarding what it judges irrelevant . . . The eye is not only an optical instrument but an electrical network which interprets what it sees'.[1] At a more complex level there exists an intriguing process known as 'the cocktail party phenomenon'. This is the type of selection which allows one to ignore the background noise of a cocktail party and carry on one's own conversation; but if someone across the room mentions one's name, this is likely to penetrate the filter so that one can attend to the comments that follow, although they are no louder than the foregoing comments which were ignored. Putting information into the black box, to return to the model given earlier, is not simply a matter of making the information accessible to the senses. The learner is not a passive recipient of information, and the teacher needs to take into account the processes of selection and attention.

Attention

Like learning itself, attention is not completely under conscious control. As the previous section has shown, much is determined at a pre-conscious level. Attention is closely related to motivation, but it would not be accurate to conclude that a student who is highly motivated by interest or fear of failure will be more attentive than one who is not so highly motivated. Strong negative motivation—fear of failure—is as likely to interfere with attention as to promote it if the task is complex. There is an optimum level of motivation for a task which depends on the complexity of the task and on the individual performing it. Strong motivation, both positive (financial) and negative (unemployment, censure) will be necessary to make a man continue to perform a simple, monotonous task such as operating a factory machine, whereas a much lower level is required for the surgeon.

Even with motivation at the best level for the specific task and individual, the span of attention is more limited than is commonly realised. In the case of a lecture, it may be possible to listen initially for ten or fifteen minutes and to resume after a break of a few seconds, but as the lecture continues these involuntary breaks in attention increase in frequency and duration until little of what is said is taken in. In an experiment by Trenaman, students who heard the first fifteen minutes of a talk were able to recall 41 per cent of the information in a subsequent test, while those who heard forty-five minutes only retained 20 per cent.[2]

The determinants of attention are to be found both in the task and in the individual. There is some evidence to suggest that the span of attention is related to the introversion-extroversion dimension of personality. Eysenck[3] carried out simple tapping tests and measured the involuntary rest pauses which demonstrate breaks in attention. The subjects were asked to tap as fast as they could for one minute—a short period, but apparently long enough to reveal a difference between introverts, who averaged one involuntary pause, and extroverts, who averaged eighteen. The fact that the task was simple and monotonous meant that attention flagged sooner than it would in an interesting lecture This factor of interest, which is related to complexity, is the task-related factor mentioned above.

Complexity is, to a large extent, inherent in the task, but there are subjective elements. A task requiring the memorising of sounds—learning to converse in a foreign language, for example—will be more difficult and appear to be more complex to someone whose memory and images are predominantly visual than to one whose images are auditory. Interest is of course a major determinant of attention, and this is almost completely subjective.

Attention, then, is not a function of intelligence but the product of a combination of factors involving motivation, personality and the nature of the task. The limitations of 'attention span' show the necessity of the selecting function.

Organisation

Looking back at the diagram given at the beginning, some of the factors influencing input have now been examined. The next stage in the learning process is organisation. Information is not inscribed in the brain like writing on a blackboard; it has to be structured, organised and related to existing knowledge. This applies at all levels of complexity. At the simple visual level, three dots on a sheet of paper may be seen to form a triangular shape although they are quite separate. A two-dimensional picture of a landscape can be 'translated' into three dimensions; this has to be learned by experience in judging distance and perspective, and is not immediately apparent to people from less sophisticated cultures, who find such pictures meaningless. Perspective was not used at all in art until about AD 1400. Later the term was used for cognitive processes

—'putting the situation in perspective'. Organisation is a vital part of the higher mental processes; ideas are linked together to form coherent conceptual systems and are examined in relation to one another. This is the basis of rational thought, though the outcome of this organisation and structuring is often far from rational.

The mind constantly seeks meaning in its precepts; this is the function of organisation. Where meaning is not apparent, a constructed meaning is imposed which may or may not then be tested against reality. This process of sorting and labelling ideas and information within the brain inevitably affects the way in which they are subsequently perceived. An example is given below.

Shape A consists of four straight lines in an approximately rectangular arrangement. Subjects were asked to memorise a number of such shapes under one of two alternative labels or names, and it was found that these labels affected the form in which the shapes were memorised and reproduced. If shape A was labelled 'hat' it would be reproduced something like shape B, if labelled 'beehive', the drawing would be more like shape C. This principle operates equally at higher cognitive levels in the organisation of ideas. Labels are often applied to categories of people according to their race or profession; in this case the labels are called stereotypes. They influence the way in which we perceive and respond to people and can help us to cope with them. Having met a bank manager or a policeman, we know to a large extent what sort of behaviour to expect from these categories of people in their professional capacity, and what sort of behaviour is expected from us.

Forming these stereotypes demands the ability to construct general principles from specific instances, and this is a type of learning which is basic to our attempts to understand and control the environment. But these principles can distort perception just as the labels affected the reproduction of the nonsense figures. One person or figure can produce totally different images according to the categories used to classify them. A racially prejudiced man going to a hospital for treatment and encountering a coloured doctor will find that his conflicting stereotypes for 'physician' and 'negro' are entirely incompatible, and he will feel confused and ambivalent towards the man, who is probably unlike either stereotype in his off-duty roles.

Stereotypes can only account for behaviour within a role; they hinder rather than help an understanding of the person who plays the role. In many cases, where relationships are impersonal, the stereotype is adequate, but within the teaching relationship it is necessary to understand some of the stereotypes of teachers which people form, as this has a profound influence on their behaviour. This will be examined later in this chapter.

Selection, attention, organisation and the search for meaning, then, are the main components of learning. If any of these stages are performed inefficiently, learning will be hindered. Organisation and the establishment of meaning are important parts of memory, but the distortion which can occur during these processes may make memory inaccurate.

Retention

For learning to take place information must be retained. At all stages of life the degree to which information is retained depends on how meaningful it is to the individual, and this is increasingly true with advancing age. Children can absorb large quantities of facts with less difficulty than adults, but it would be an oversimplification to say that memory deteriorates with age. In order to explore the effects of age on memory, it is necessary to distinguish at first between two kinds of meaning, intrinsic and extrinsic.

A verse of a poem is more intrinsically meaningful than a list containing the same number of words taken at random from a dictionary, for there is a greater probability of one word occurring in association with another in the poem. 'Blue', for example, is more likely to be followed by 'sky' than by 'hippopotamus'. The more intrinsically meaningful information is, the easier it is to learn. Poetry is easier to learn by heart than prose, and prose is easier than a list of random words. But there is also the question of extrinsic meaning, which does not lie in the information but in the hearer. A news item about Bolivia, for example, will be remembered by someone who has visited it, but rapidly forgotten by anyone who has hardly heard of the place. Intrinsically, the news item has the same degree of meaning for them both, but there is a great difference in extrinsic meaning.

For the child, intrinsic meaning is the primary form. Information must be simple and coherent. There appears to be something satisfying in rhythm and repetition to the young child, who enjoys hearing the same stories many times and is likely to protest if the wording is changed. Children's games make use of well-defined rhymes whose rhythm seems more important than their wording. Children have a facility for accumulating information on diverse unrelated topics and their interests develop and change from day to day. Adults are less flexible and for them extrinsic meaning is of primary importance. An adult will be more likely to study a difficult book on a topic that has long been of interest to him than an easy text on a subject he has never encountered before. Adults do, of course, take up new subjects, but it appears to be more difficult for them to do so than for a child who learns new things every day. Adult life (to oversimplify matters for the sake of brevity) can be seen as the period when specialisation becomes easier than diversification. How far this is inherent in human nature and how far it is artificially conditioned by an educational system geared to selection for university entrance is not known. It will be interesting to see how theories of adult learning change as it becomes normal for a man to embark on a new career several times during his life, as his skills become obsolete.

There is a certain amount of physiological evidence to support the idea that adulthood is a time for reinforcing skills and abilities rather than for innovation. The physiological psychologist Hebb concluded that adulthood is concerned with 'a strengthening of facilitations, not a setting up of new connections between wholly unrelated activities.' After maturity, brain cells die off and can never be replaced, but fortunately only a small proportion of the total are ever used and the interconnections between the cells develop into an increasingly complex network which for many years more than compensates for this decline in numbers. If it is easier to make connections between cells already in use than to call upon the waning reserves of 'spare' cells, it would seem logical that specialisation should come more easily to the adult than innovation.

The physicist, for example, may continue to research into his special aspect of the subject until he knows more about it than anyone else, but his memory of the elements of physics outside his personal field is likely to weaken. He may also find it more difficult to keep up with current affairs, though his vocabulary is likely to continue its development. One general principle which emerges is that a brain which is kept active preserves its network of interconnections longer than an inactive brain, so the effects of ageing are not entirely beyond voluntary control. This is of particular relevance to adult educators.

LEARNING IN THE CLASSROOM

The rational, logical components of learning described in the previous section may be seen as the tip of the iceberg which represents learning; a far greater proportion lies beneath the surface, unseen and less accessible. In a learning situation it is the whole person who experiences and reacts, not the logical black box, and to examine adult learning in the classroom it is necessary to explore some of the other psychological processes which are involved. This may be done by looking back over the six categories dealt with in the first part of the chapter and focusing on the relation of the learner to the teacher.

Retention

Attitudes to the teacher may be examined in the light of early experience retained in the memory of the adult. Because almost everyone has had both good and bad teachers, attitudes towards members of this profession are likely to polarise into two opposing categories which may exist side by side in the same person. Inconsistencies are not uncommon in human attitudes, and these give rise to the mixed feelings known as ambivalence.

It has been stated that events and information of personal relevance to the student are retained. This may include experiences which he would prefer to forget. In the long process of education mistakes are inevitable, and there can be few people who have not been made to feel small by a teacher at school. Memories inaccessible to the conscious mind but emanating from the deeper pre-conscious levels may still be of influence. Parents going to visit their children's schools may find themselves waiting outside the headmaster's door with the chill feeling in the stomach associated with the discovery of some childhood misdemeanour, though they know they have no need to be apprehensive in the present situation. This reveals that in some part of their mind is an association of unpleasant ideas connected with school.

Organisation

Early in infancy the child organises his experiences so that the 'good mother' who protects and nurtures him is differentiated from the 'bad mother' who imposes restrictions and prohibitions which frustrate his need to explore. This is because the child cannot reconcile these experiences as relating to the same person; he needs to organise in terms of black and white. His early experience with a teacher may be similarly polarised; later, when he has known both good and bad teachers, this early framework will be built on.

Since the child cannot look after himself, he experiences a need for the protection and security provided by a powerful, omniscient and benign parent-figure. Dependency in childhood produces a need for reassurance from someone who knows the answers to all problems. Parents and teachers are often seen in this role by children, and it is part of the process of growing up to realise that these people are human and therefore fallible, subject to all the irritations of the world and unable to provide all the answers. This is a disillusioning experience for the child who, after accepting that parents are fallible, may cling to a belief in a teacher. Some people never come to terms with teachers as human beings and will be disturbed in adulthood to encounter a teacher who is democratic rather than authoritarian. They will probably be unable to explain why, even to themselves, but it is because the teacher did not live up to the idealised stereotype of omniscience.

The opposite stereotype, the 'bad teacher', is compounded of frustrations encountered in conflict with both parents as well as with teachers. All the attributes of the 'bad mother', who in supervising and protecting must inevitably restrain and frustrate the child, may be projected on to the teacher who imposes some prohibition. The imposition of an impersonal authority whose criteria for judgement are incomprehensible may be attributed to the teacher as well as the father. Both these people are representatives of the unknown world outside the reassuring relationship with the mother. This may make adults who are normally well-balanced unduly sensitive to any criticism from someone in a teaching role. How these situations are dealt with will depend on the individual teacher; there is no universal prescription, but an awareness of the problems likely to arise in teaching adults, and an understanding of the origins of these problems, is a good basis for the development of social skills in the teaching situation.

Attention

Now that the limitations of attention have been described, it remains to indicate how the teacher may make allowances for this and minimise fatigue. The old adage 'tell them what you intend to say, say it, and then tell them what you have said' is appropriate to a certain extent. While attention is at its peak at the beginning of a lesson, it is as well to outline the ground that is supposed to be covered, so that when attention later lapses, as it inevitably does, the listener may more easily pick up the thread. When one channel of communication is fatigued—in other words, when the audience begin to tire of listening—it helps to use another channel for a while. Audio-visual aids may be introduced, or some practical demonstration where appropriate, or an illustration may be made on the blackboard. If a complex point has to be made towards the end of a lesson when attention is flagging, it will have to be made in more detail than would have been necessary for the same point at the beginning of the lesson. A summary at the end may be more fruitful than the section on attention implied, for awareness that the lesson is nearing its end tends to have a revivifying effect, and so the contents of the final minutes have a reasonable chance of retention. The summary must be brief, however, for repetition of over-familiar material can cause a complete failure of attention.

C

Selection

Like attention, this process is not entirely under voluntary control. It is not always possible to filter out extraneous information, and one may leave a lecture with more vivid impressions of the hardness of the seat or the colours of the lecturer's tie than of the subject of his discourse. Selection of the appropriate points for retention increases in difficulty with the unfamiliarity of the subject-matter. To the trained mind of the teacher the salient points may appear obvious, but the student has more difficulty in separating the central from the peripheral. It will usually facilitate selection if some framework of the ground to be covered is given to the class before beginning the course, or at the start of the lesson, as mentioned earlier. This may take the form of a printed handout or a list of headings on the board. Then, when attention lapses, as it does several times in the course of the lesson, it will be easier for the student to reorientate himself and select the relevant points instead of floundering and being unable to follow the argument.

Imagery

On reading the section on imagery the reader may feel, that it is impossible for him to make adequate provision for the wide range of individual differences described. Again, awareness of the problem is the first step in coping with it and there are no universal prescriptions for successful communication, but this is an area in which the diversity of the audience may be useful to the teacher. Few people are aware of the possible range of imagery, for formal education tends to channel awareness into only two senses, vision and hearing, so that people who learn best by tactile and kinaesthetic operations are often dismissed as lacking academic ability. This is not necessarily so; it may reflect the shortcomings of the system rather than the inadequacies of the pupil. There are people, for instance, who remain indifferent to poetry until a visit to the Lake District gives them an insight into Wordsworth. The discovery of individual differences in imagery usually provokes a lively discussion, and looking at different ways of conceptualising an idea is one way to facilitate learning. A moderate-sized class will often contain one person who experiences synesthesia—a linking of two or more sensory channels so that a number, for example, may always be associated with a colour, or the music of Bach may be 'seen' in geometric patterns. An awareness of these different modes of imagery may be useful as well as interesting, as it may encourage the development of new learning techniques. Often people are not initially aware of their particular type of imagery; this can be discovered by eliciting their associations with some familiar situation—for instance, eating breakfast—to see if they think in terms of visual images, sounds, smells or movement.

The Senses

The only general principle to emerge from this study of the senses is that their acuity tends to decrease with age. The provision that the adult teacher may make for this is to present his material to as many of the senses as possible; this also makes allowances for individual differences in sensory predominance and makes attention easier by avoiding the overburdening of one channel. There is no one way of communicating with everyone; a picture is not necessarily 'worth a thousand words', though people who learn better by reading and seeing than by being told things may be expected to benefit less from a lecture than others. Some things can only be learned by experiencing them; social processes such as group dynamics, the sound of an engine with a specific defect, or the effects of schizophrenia on personality, for example. The classroom situation is limited in the learning experiences it can furnish, but an awareness of the nature of these limitations will enable the adult teacher to make the best use of the potentialities.

NOTES

1   Bronowski, J. *The Identity of Man* (1967), 31
2   BBC Further Education Experiment. *The Length of a Talk* (1951)
3   Eysenck, H. J. *Fact and Fiction in Psychology* (1967)

FURTHER READING

Miller, H. L. *Teaching and Learning in Adult Education* (1964)
Gagne, R. *The Conditions of Learning* (New York 1966)
Hunter, I. *Memory* (1964)
Borger, R. and Seaborne, A. E. M. *The Psychology of Learning* (1964)
Cleugh, M. F. *Educating Older People* (1962)

3 Relationships Within Adult Classes

Derek Legge

SOME GENERAL QUESTIONS AND PROBLEMS

There are frequent assertions that relationships within adult classes are of vital importance to the success or failure of the work, but the evidence supporting these seems to be almost entirely subjective. This is not to assert that they are necessarily false but merely to introduce a note of caution before looking further at a highly complex subject.

The kind of importance, moreover, is not always clear. Is it just the need of the teacher for self-esteem or is it an essential feature of satisfactory learning? Other questions need to be asked. Is there a relationship between the teacher and the whole class or only a series of relationships between him and individual members? Do relationships between students matter at all? How far is it possible to generalise about relationships in adult classes which differ so widely? Is it, for example, true that one type of relationship is better for non-examination classes in liberal studies, while a quite different type would be preferable in a class in a technical subject leading to a professional examination and qualification? What difference does it make if the teacher is also an assessor or examiner? Do 'good' relationships imply that the teacher should be all things to all men or that he should have exactly the same kind of relationship with each student? Is the latter even a possibility?

In this chapter relationships will be discussed in terms of the possible contribution they can make to student learning and an attempt will be made to bring together current views about 'the right relationships'. In many ways these centre upon ideas about the status and role of the teacher, about desirable characteristics, about the contributions of personality and temperament and about the effects of human interaction in an adult class. Visits to adult classes soon indicate that there are wide variations in the ideas which are held by teachers of adults about these matters, and indeed sometimes contradictions between the ideas and practice, but even so it seems possible to extract a number of common factors which are important for most classes.

Before turning to these it is valuable to recognise that relationships in adult classes are the product of many factors, some of which are not within the control of the teacher. His opinions, attitudes and views— in a real sense his whole philosophy of life—are of course important, but so too are the opinions and views of the students. They may wish to invest the teacher with authority and to establish a subservient relationship whether he likes it or not. Indeed, in many parts of the world a long tradition suggests that it is desirable to 'sit at the feet of the master', and adult students often arrive with a view of what the right relationship should be which may be in conflict with that of the teacher. Similarly, relationships are influenced by the circumstances under which the class meets, by the degree of compulsion over attendance, by the way in which the class is organised, and by the degree of heterogeneity in the student groups. A group with a great range of ages, social background, previous educational experience etc may present problems of relationships quite different from the relatively homogeneous group with a narrow age range as seen, for example, in many day release classes in colleges of further education. The type of subject matter also conditions relationships; where the material is mainly factual the teacher may be cast as a didactic provider of knowledge, whereas when it is more controversial he may experience pressure to be on more equal terms with his students. Environmental factors have their influence. It is difficult for the teacher to be 'one among equals' when he is placed on a dais or has to teach from the well of a lecture theatre with fixed tiered seats. One may speculate a good deal about the relationships in a class which met in an old court house wherein the teacher occupied the dock, although in practice it seemed that the humour of the situation helped the success of the class not a little.

RELATIONSHIPS BETWEEN TEACHER AND STUDENT

In most types of adult class the status of the teacher is different from that of a teacher of children in a school. Obviously he is not superior in size or physical power, and frequently he has little of the authority emanating from a school as an established institution. Even in the technical college or college of further education there is little support for the schoolmastering tradition, especially in these days of growing 'student power'. In evening institutes, WEA, or extra-mural classes, the teacher often finds himself younger than his students, perhaps inferior in social position, and often with a non-captive group which if it wishes can leave him unemployed. Ideas about teacher's power may well receive salutary shocks in a class which, even if it does not openly voice its disapproval, may 'vote with its feet' and not be present the following week. In non-examination classes, real power rests with the students, and any authority which they choose to recognise in the teacher will be granted only on two counts: his knowledge of the subject and his ability to help the students learn.

This recognition that the position and status of a teacher in an adult class depends upon his merits and ability provides some clues to the type of relationship which seem to be most helpful. The traditional view in liberal study classes is that equality is the most desirable type of relationship, but it is clear that, strictly speaking, this is not achievable. Students would not come to a class in which the teacher knew only as much as they did. As Brian Groombridge has noted, 'tutor and students know that they are not equal: their presence together depends on a recognition that they are not equal'. A teacher's superiority in skills and teaching ability, however, must not extend to superiority in other qualities, and it is of vital importance for him to recognise that, apart from his own specialisation, he may well be inferior to his students and could learn from them. Even in terms of specialist knowledge or skills, no teacher knows all of his subject and a student may be able to add something new. If this happens it should be recognised as right and proper within an adult class. Tawney used to say that he learnt his economic history from his Rochdale and Longton tutorial classes, and most teachers of adults are aware that in a very real sense they learn more in the class than do their students. Provided the teacher recognises that he is not a superior being, it seems clear that, though remaining the central figure, he can with advantage seek a more relaxed relationship.

The advantage of this must be measured, however, in terms of its effect on adult learning, and it is here that difficulties are encountered. The relatively small number of experiments which have tried to test the question are far from conclusive and indeed seem to suggest that what matters is the degree of compatibility between the teacher's and students' views of the desired relationship. If both teacher and students want a rather cold, distant relationship, with the teacher as a somewhat remote and exalted figure, then it would seem that learning is just as effective as in a class where both teacher and students want a warm, friendly atmosphere, close and happy relationships, with the teacher as a permissive, understanding figure. Rarely, of course, do all the students have such unanimity of viewpoint, although in non-examination classes the drop-out of those who do not like the prevailing trend in relationships may produce a greater degree of homogeneity. Few would want to see adult classes treated like infants in nineteenth-century schools, but a class has been known to retain most of its members throughout a whole winter despite a teacher who told them when to pick up their pens and when to lay them down.

The key to this lies in the need to reduce emotional tension if satisfactory learning is to take place. Thus some students may find their anxieties increased by the teacher who abdicates authority and seeks a relationship of 'all friends together'. Some may want authoritative guidance, or may want 'to be taught' or to be reassured or even disciplined by a superior being. It may be argued that these students show immaturity and adolescent dependence and that the teacher should seek to change the situation, but this is not something which can be done with haste, and most students display these attitudes at one time or another in their adult life. Moreover, if adult students want quick results in terms of learning, as many do, they may well demand that the teacher gives them the knowledge 'from on high' without worrying about relationships. Some very mature members of adult classes have been known to show considerable irritation at what they have regarded as a waste of time when a teacher has tried to establish the relationship, so often advocated, of equality, friendliness and warmth. 'My time is limited; let us get on with the job', may be a limited view but it is one that teachers of adult classes on occasion may have to respect, especially in classes which are leading towards examinations.

With this caution, however, it seems to be true that for *most* adult students in *most* adult classes, learning is made easier if the teacher can foster relationships which cause the class to be more of a community working together than a collection of individuals competitively seeking the fulfilment of their own personal desires. A teacher in any class can satisfy only a small fraction of student needs, and tensions must increase unless it becomes easy for the students to speak out freely about the subject, the general situation and its problems. In general the teacher's task may be viewed as that of releasing the full powers of class members, of helping them to reduce their inhibitions and emotional blockages, and for most students this is more likely to happen if the teacher is an understanding, accepting person, respectful as well as respected, in a group which has attained both freedom and a social stability built on cohesion, not coercion. This appears to be true just as much of examination classes as of others.

Thinking of teachers in general, S. Wiseman[1] drew attention to the value in teaching of understanding, friendly behaviour in contrast to aloof, egocentric behaviour, and of stimulating, imaginative, enthusiastic behaviour in contrast to dull routine behaviour, and this seems particularly applicable to adult classes. Of Tawney in 1908 it was said that he: 'won the affection and confidence of his class from the outset',[2] that he 'possessed the faculty of being able to capture and to hold the interest of his class' and that above all 'he showed himself to be an enthusiast in the work, and no trouble was too much for him'.

The argument is that most adult classes seem to achieve better results and to learn better if there is a relationship in which co-operation is paramount and with it the students' feelings of personal worth, acceptance and security. How to achieve this, however, remains a problem. Some would say that it depends entirely on the personality of the teacher and are tempted to devise long, extravagant statements about the qualities of the good teacher. One often wonders how the paragons of virtue in these statements manage to survive in a real world. Others put their faith in the arrangement of furniture in the room, in the introduction of a sociable tea-break, in social activities outside the class, in the virtues of arriving early and departing late so that there can be informal discussions with individuals or small groups. All these may be found to be helpful, although how far they are piacticable depends upon the type of course. A short crash course is obviously different from a regular one night per week course, and residential courses present different possibilities from those in non-residential adult education. Perhaps inevitably we are back to the importance of the teacher's manner and approach in the development of human relationships, and at the risk of projecting personal likes and dislikes it may be suggested that the following characteristics seem to be generally helpful to effective relationships and through them to student learning.

Perhaps of first importance is the development of a *sensitivity* to the class and to the individuals who compose it. In some ways this is difficult to express in words. It is a kind of sympathetic, imaginative understanding of the students, an ability to sense what they are thinking or feeling, what their needs, difficulties and problems are. It implies patience, tact, diplomacy, above all a need to know as much as possible about students, and also some attempt by the teacher to see himself as they see him. Adult students rightly size up the teacher as much as he tries to weigh up their possibilities, and although no one can really put himself into the mind of another, the willing attempt to do so leads often to mutual respect and an approach which casts aside superior attitudes, sarcasm, ridicule or patronage. Perhaps this characteristic is best described as a genuine interest in other people, a desire to identify the needs of others, and a recognition of common humanity with all its strengths and weaknesses.

Secondly, a certain *humility* helps relationships. It has been said that pride is the besetting sin of all teachers, and even though, as indicated above, the teacher in most classes will have a superior knowledge of the subject, he needs to resist the temptation to pretend to know all about all matters. If a relationship based on mutual trust and confidence is developing, students will often turn to the teacher for advice on matters well outside the subject of study, and even within the subject he may well need to say 'I don't know'. Within the class, in fact, he must accept the same discipline that he requires from his students, and frequently this means a patient acceptance of criticism, the admission of error, confessions of ignorance and a tolerance of differences, especially in subjects which allow for alternative answers. He should indeed know his own limitations and how little he can achieve in the limited contact he has with students, and he should not be afraid to let this become apparent. A sense of humour clearly contributes much.

This humility must, of course, be genuine and not contrived. Students will indeed only come to trust a teacher who they feel has *integrity and sincerity,* and they will respect him for what he is and for the standards he sets himself. Integrity implies not only accuracy in the presentation of information but also scrupulous fairness and at times resistance to the demands of students. At times adult students want speedy answers, 'prefabricated' by the teacher, who may well have to indicate that even provisional answers to problems need sustained and serious study, and that students can only really come to a knowledge of the subject by their own efforts. At these points of apparent conflict between the wishes of the students and the integrity of the teacher, the value of a close, friendly relationship based upon mutual respect becomes most apparent. Similarly, when it is important to set standards in, for example, skills, tension is likely to develop when the student fears criticism from the aloof teacher, whereas he may well be reassured and encouraged to try again when he has a relationship of trust and freedom.

Lastly, a useful dividend seems to result from the *enthusiasm* of the teacher. Perhaps enthusiasm is not the best word. This characteristic does not imply flamboyance, noise or energy, but rather an intense personal belief that the work is worth while, that the subject is of vital interest and that it is of supreme importance to give of one's best in helping the growth of others. In a classroom it shows itself often as an intensive man-to-man contact involving both personality and knowledge of the subject, and a willingness to spare no effort in trying to help the students. It implies, of course, working closely with the class, and a certain tenacity which leads the teacher to renewed effort even though he is often aware of his failures and inevitable insufficiency to achieve the aims he sets for himself. In this way the enthusiasm is linked to himself and to integrity.

RELATIONSHIPS BETWEEN STUDENTS

In recent years more attention has been paid to the importance of group relationships in furthering the development of adult learning, and reference to this is made elsewhere in this book.[3] It is worth noting, however, that for over a century in Britain some types of adult education have stressed the value of social coherence in the adult class, and have usually described this as 'fellowship'. We find it from the mid-nineteenth century onwards in the working men's colleges and in the new type adult schools after the work of Sturge, as well as in the later Workers' Educational Association. Basically 'fellowship' implies that a class becomes a community in which ideas and information are shared and work is done on a basis of co-operation rather than competition. In terms of adult learning this seems to produce greater satisfaction and hence better assimilation of subject matter. By removing or reducing potential threats in the class environment, it also reduces emotional tension. Many adults feel ill at ease in their first class meeting; some because of earlier educational experiences which are associated with unpleasantness, but most because in the new untried situation they are defensive, oversensitive to possible challenge by their fellow students, and unwilling to expose what they regard as their ignorance and lack of ability. Emotionally they need acceptance and security in order to be able to learn, and this can only be achieved in a group which accords to each a recognition of personal worth.

The negative aspects of poor relationships between students in a class are more easily seen than the positive ones. When a group is divided into virtually two or more warring camps, energy is deflected from learning. Similarly, a dominant clique which tries to monopolise the attention of the teacher—or indeed sometimes to take over his work—can intensify inferiority feelings among the others and increase the emotional barriers. 'If those members can grasp the subject so quickly and so well, then I must indeed be dull and incapable' is a thought which is by no means infrequent. Both the outer and the inner group will tend to defend their emotionally established positions and to resist the changes which learning requires. If the teacher should have good relations with one group and not with the other the problem is aggravated.

Sometimes groups develop a coherence because of the work of their own members, for example when a class secretary is chosen and carries out his work conscientiously. More often, however, the teacher must consciously plan ways of achieving the desired group relationship. As suggested earlier, this may be aided by attention to physical conditions, seating etc, by arranging opportunities for general conversation before or after the class meeting, by organised out-of-class activities and by the now more customary tea-break. What has to be realised is that relationships are not fixed or static, that they change with each meeting of the class, and that they need to be fostered throughout a course. The teacher, however, is not a manipulator pulling strings; he requires the help of all members to be really successful in securing those relationships which are most conducive to learning. Good teaching stems from the teacher's ability to channel productively the interests, needs, capacities and hopes of his students, and the more the student feels satisfaction in relationships and acceptance and significance in the group, the more likely it is that he will achieve the desired educational objectives. Adults need security as well as stimulus if they are to continue learning in a satisfactory way. Ideally they should have this in their relationship both with the teacher and with their companions.

NOTES

1 Wiseman, S. 'Characteristics of Successful Teachers', *Memoirs & Proceedings of the Manchester Literary & Philosophical Society,* 105 (1962-3)
2 Reports on First Tutorial Classes at Longton and Rochdale, in *Oxford and Working Class Education* (Oxford 1908), Appendix, 104-8
3 See Ch 2

FURTHER READING

Burmeister, W. 'The Tutor's Qualities', *Adult Education,* 26 no 1 (1953)
Cleugh, M. F. *Educating Older People* (1962), Ch 7
Highet, G. *The Art of Teaching* (1951)
Kidd, J. R. *How Adults Learn* (New York 1959), Ch 11
Peers, R. *Adult Education: A Comparative Study* (1958), Ch 10
Raybould, S. G. *The Approach to W.E.A. Teaching* (1947)
Ruddock, R. 'The Psychology of Psychologists', *Highway,* 43 (1951-2)
Sprott, W. J. H. *Human Groups* (1958)
Styler, W. E. (ed). *The Good Tutor: A Student View* (Manchester 1956)

4 Syllabus Design and Lesson Preparation

David Connor

SYLLABUS DESIGN

Traditional Approaches

T he problem of student unrest is not to be found in the world of non-vocational adult education, despite the ferment of reappraisal common to much of the educational world. In Britain this must in part be due to the absence of any rigidity on the part of the providing bodies and the Department of Education and Science. Increasingly attempts are being made to overcome the educationally false division between the practically based and appreciation-type courses, between the concrete and the abstract. This presents a challenge to teachers and administrators and will make new demands on accommodation and equipment as well as on future syllabus and lesson preparation. Syllabuses in general reflect the interest of the student. It is, however, in the main true to say that there has been no break with traditional approaches since the inception of the Workers' Educational Association at the turn of the century, although there have been several waves of criticism and a trend towards a more realistic and analytical approach. Such changes in syllabus content as we observe have been the result of a continuous attempt to take in new topics as they arose or to reflect changing attitudes to traditional material.

Why a Syllabus?

The syllabus can only be a reflection of the prior thinking about the form and content of the course which has been undertaken by the teacher. The main purpose is to clarify the subject matter to be studied and to show how it will be approached. It can at the same time be seen as a form of remote control over the composition of the class to be recruited. While the main purpose is to interest and attract the student most likely to benefit from the course, it is at the same time important to be aware that one is rejecting certain students through the content and orientation of the syllabus.

The only tangible evidence of what the student is about to **undertake** is the piece of paper which outlines the course. When there is no material inducement in the form of a certificate or diploma at the end of this commitment to a class (which also involves time for reading, preparation and often considerable travel) the importance of the syllabus to the student is apparent. Apart from setting out the aims and acting as a guide to the general shape of the course, it should be possible for the student to refer back as the course proceeds in order to see the way in which his knowledge has developed.

When the potential student comes to the enrolment centre to consult this document it is often surprising that he decides to commit himself on the basis of this sheet of paper, let alone to part with his money. The visitor to the office of the providing body invariably requires more information than the title or synopsis can give and the organiser is dependent on the syllabus to help the student in this all-important decision.

For Whom?

If the answer to this question were known on every occasion a class was arranged, advertising problems would be solved. On the face of it, selecting a title appears to be a simple matter. In fact it is undoubtedly the first determinant of class recruitment. The teacher is as involved in this dilemma as the organiser and is better placed, with his first-hand knowledge of the course, to devote time and thought to devising a title than is the providing body which may be arranging several hundred courses.

Titles are probably as difficult as any aspect of syllabus preparation and should be attractive, bearing in mind that they are sometimes used for publicity purposes without any synopsis. The title must be brief for printing and yet has to convey to the potential student what the course is about. Once one departs from using the formal academic title it is difficult to convey speedily the content of the course and yet it is vitally important to attempt to find an original title which succeeds in being attractive.

While the syllabus is read by those responsible for providing the course, and in the case of the responsible bodies goes to the Inspector, they will only read it from the student viewpoint. Ideally students should be able to discuss the syllabus with the teacher before the course is provided. All too often this proves impossible and the syllabus is in fact an advertising medium for the class. For this very reason it should be open to amendment and modification in the light of the students' wishes.

As one of the cardinal tenets is consultation with the students, it is very desirable that the teacher should ask the organising body for any information it has about the potential students and their needs. This is unfortunately not always available, but in specific instances such as courses for trade unions, Townswomen's Guilds, or community associations it is possible to ascertain the precise needs of the students and their background. It is important to gain an idea of the educational attainment, age, sex, social class and any other facts known to the organisers. When a class is being taken over, the reports and register should be consulted and discussed with the previous teacher where this is possible.

Aims and Planning

The syllabus, apart from being a summary of the ground to be covered, should give the main topics in a logical order which will show the inter-relationships which exist between the various parts being dealt with. The problem is how to balance these aspects without superficiality on the one hand or an excess of pedantry on the other. One should not underestimate the considerable effort required in order to achieve success in this. The outcome of discussion with the student may mean modification, but the need for discipline in the interest of an academically sound programme will be readily accepted by the student.

The length of the course is a decisive factor in planning the shape of the syllabus, and, while the shorter course will be devoted to a concise treatment of an aspect of a subject, it is unwise to assume that the longer course can do so much more. It is often not appreciated, even by those engaged in teaching subjects within the field of liberal studies, that the same systematic build-up has to be undertaken as for a technical course. The problem is how to convince the student that the seemingly uninteresting but essential stages are worth while. The philosopher who wishes his students to obtain a grasp of logic will need to use skilful and persuasive ways with most adult groups.

While a highly selective syllabus is necessary for the student to exercise his critical faculties, a problem arises when balancing this with the demand for more general coverage of the field. Fresh approaches to knowledge are possible when adults seek to study some social or political question which may involve historical, geographical, technological or other inter-disciplinary fields of learning.

Format—Words and Clarity

After being presented with a multitude of syllabuses I am convinced that the need for a standard yardstick is self-evident. Generally the syllabus should be written with people in mind who know little or nothing about the subject. Simplicity and clarity are the essential elements and are worth mentioning even though they seem obvious. There can be a tendency to carry distaste for the methods of the advertising world to such an extent that dreary and involved presentation is thought to be a virtue.

It is best to write the syllabus with a specific student in mind. Much of the failure to attract students from a wider background than that common to the majority of adult educational classes is in part due to the type of language used in synopses and syllabuses. Use of jargon should be avoided unless the students have previously reached a standard of work which necessitates a technical vocabulary; it is surprising how frequently a simpler alternative can be found. A conscious effort may be required to avoid the over-latinised vocabulary common to many teachers. Paragraphs should not be unduly long, and actual layout of the page can be varied in a manner which makes it more easily read.

Content—Selection and Organisation

All too often the most sketchy outline is presented as a syllabus, clear evidence of lack of thought and preparation, and, one fears, failure to attach importance to the task itself. This not infrequently happens even with teachers whose flair for adult education and knowledge of their subject is considerable. There is a difficulty in pioneering courses, when the teacher knows the risk of the class not materialising (which incidentally is a hazard for all providing bodies), but this must not diminish the care taken in preparation. At the other extreme is over-preparation, perhaps most common among less experienced teachers. A frequent result of this is a syllabus presented in the form of itemised and numbered points which proves to be a strait-jacket both for the teacher and his students.

The whole development of a subject from classical to contemporary times in twenty or twenty-four weeks is quite frequently suggested, and even were it possible to race through in this way it is clearly undesirable to skim the surface. Reflection will soon show that the study in depth of a specific period or aspect of the subject will be of more lasting benefit for the student and will enable him to apply himself more effectively to other aspects later. It may not be necessary to go to the lengths of a philosopher who will use one text for the whole session, but that extreme is far preferable to superficiality in treatment. In the main it would appear best to restrict longer courses to a few major texts. There should be no difficulty in introducing new subject matter as opportunity arises or as the students' own interest and abilities emerge, but far more lasting satisfaction will arise from having ably mastered a major work, be it a play by Shakespeare, Ayer's *Language, Truth and Logic,* or the works of a given period of a composer. New methods of presentation should be sought. Why not work back from the known to the unknown? There is no reason why the historical approach should be in chronological order. A course currently offered, 'Music before Bach', works from the familiar into the less well known by moving backwards historically, and doubtless will draw parallels from the earlier period to the later developments of today, which in many ways are more akin to the pre-harmonic period than to the days of classical tonality.

Booklists—Libraries

It is most important to direct students to original sources of material. It is also important to ensure that the latest texts and references are given to them, as so often in adult education they have come to the teacher in order to discover the latest thought in his subject. This does not mean that more recent works should necessarily be preferred to older ones. If the teacher is not a member of a university staff it is always possible, through the university extra-mural department library, a public library or the national central library to obtain the latest material. Personal contact with the librarian of the public library is always welcomed, and is advisable well before the course begins in order to ascertain the availability of the books required. Specialist advice related to adult education is most likely to be available from the librarian of a university extra-mural department.

In general, booklists should be short and appropriate to the anticipated academic level, as very long lists tend to overwhelm students. The list should be related to the stages of development indicated in the syllabus, or supplementary lists may be given to students as the course progresses. Care should be taken to avoid the tendency to select over-specialised titles which will predominate in the teacher's own reading. It is important to ensure that the library receives the full list before the beginning of the course. It is sensible to encourage students to acquire their own copies, especially as paperbacks are so readily available. Indeed the teacher will often be called upon to play the role of adviser on 'library building'. It is also important to ensure that books are available from the library source or cheaply in paperbacks, and in many instances it is preferable to obtain sets.

The booklist is inseparable from the syllabus and is primarily a guide for the student to follow in his out-of-class preparation. Helpful comments indicating specially important books, those suitable for beginners, chapters of a book or certain sections of relevance to the course, may be briefly made.

As the list will be used by the librarian, it is essential to give full and accurate details preferably in the following order: author's name, initials, full title, publisher, date of publication. An indication of the availability of cheap editions and their price will also help the students. Distinction should be made between books for essential reading, books for reference and more general books, and also between the various levels of difficulty. Their availability and the requirements of the library should be discussed with the providing body or the librarian. Supplementary lists can always be added as the course progresses, but it is essential to bear in mind that libraries are inundated with requests just before the opening of a session and that early lists stand a far better chance of attention.

Particular care is needed over the specification of periodical articles and of contributions to collective works. It is not unknown for these to be specified as though they were books. Periodical articles should be quoted under the name of the journal or periodical, with date and volume number. Contributions to collective works should be quoted under the name of the collection and its editor. When recommended works are likely to prove difficult to obtain, the teacher should approach the appropriate public or institutional libraries, so that arrangements may be put in hand, eg for the temporary loan of rare works through the regional library systems or the National Central Library, for photostat copies to be made of periodical articles, or for copies of poems and similar material to be duplicated for class use. It is desirable that libraries should be consulted at an early stage (before booklists are prepared) so that any additions to stock, by purchase or loan, may be made.

Teachers should bear in mind that the inclusion of a title on a list of recommended reading may provoke a multiple demand. They need also to be reminded that students take their recommendations seriously, and that many develop an almost pathological concern to obtain the books that their teacher recommends. The importance of reading lists to students, and their resultant effect upon libraries and booksellers should not be underrated.

LESSON PREPARATION

Adapting the Syllabus to Student Needs

If the syllabus is the plan for the course it does not obviate the need to plan for each individual class meeting. The first requirement is for the teacher to be student-orientated. In general, the teacher who is entirely absorbed in his subject and has no interest in people is unlikely to succeed as an educator. The planning of the individual meetings, as well as the design of the syllabus, can often be done with the students, so that they can participate in the drawing up of a plan of campaign.

Adequate time should be devoted to discussion of the syllabus and adapting it to the expectations and potentialities of the students when they meet the teacher. The adult generally prefers a clear sense of purpose and aim in undertaking a course, and a vague approach by the teacher is not likely to inspire high standards in the student. Lesson preparation calls for a scheme for the teacher to work to, and this may be seen as separate from the syllabus itself or indeed as a second syllabus. It is useful for the teacher to have an outline of his course and to have a target for each session so that he can measure progress.

While it is out of the question for the average adult student and lay-man to obtain the skills and techniques of the specialist, and it is not the aim to obtain an encyclopaedic knowledge, it is desirable that there should be an opportunity to give the framework and criteria of the dis-cipline in order to understand the mental processes and outlook which are the distinctive features of the professional. It can be quite fascinating to see the similarities between different disciplines; for example, an architect studying music found constant surprise at the number of con-ceptual forms which lay behind musical development and the thought processes which paralleled those in his own field of creative design. It is unlikely that the student can make any contribution to the speciality, yet the specialist may often gain from the interests of someone who is versed in another speciality or from the experience of someone who is able to throw a new light on the subject matter.

Successful discussion will depend on forethought; a number of ques-tions related to various parts of the lecture may be thrown out in the course of discussion, but self-restraint may be necessary to avoid deliver-ing a second lecture. It should be discussion, not question and answer, except in purely factual matters. Care must always be taken not to give a student a sense of inferiority, and there is a challenge in finding a skilful answer to a stupid question. Until a group is known to a teacher it is very dangerous to direct a question to any particular individual.

Awareness of Variables and Student Individuality

The academic standards of the early school-leaver are often dis-paraged, yet many clergy and social workers in touch with young adults today comment on their greater general knowledge, awareness and sophistication. Undoubtedly the growth of the mass media, as well as their schooling, has some part to play in this. What I wish to stress is the need for an empathy with the student based on an awareness of the individual background. Progress can only be made by taking these factors into account.

A useful work on the language barrier is *Social Class, Language and Education* by Denis Lawton, which summarises the work in this field, includes a critique of Bernstein's important work, and also contains a useful bibliography on the subject.

Planning for Student Participation

An interesting handbook was produced by Dr. Bayliss for Nottingham University Department of Adult Education entitled *The Standard of*

Living, which was used as an integral part of the first experiment in this country of combining television, a correspondence course, and meetings of students and teachers. The weekly exercises were divided into sections with true or false statements to be answered by placing a T. or F. in the appropriate box, a section of multiple choice with various statements which required a tick, and a final section subdivided into various topics or questions which required answers of varying lengths. Methods such as these may be used when there is difficulty in obtaining written work, and often asking the student for material for a project will gain a response where a direct request for an essay would be ignored. It is often useful to devise a set of questions related to aspects of one topic and then to set small groups to discuss and work on these before pooling their results with the class as a whole. Research projects for small groups of three or four, using reference or historical sections of a library, for example, will speed the student on the way to learning how to use sources far more effectively than informing him about the process.

While there is often value in running a class with a broad range of ability and previous knowledge, there is no doubt that the approach required by a graduate in the study of a new subject will differ from that of the student who left school at fifteen, and one cannot presume, in all students who attend, the broad basic education which has a grasp of the fundamentals of the various disciplines. Students need encouragement and advice on note-taking, and it is good policy to encourage them to keep a folder for their notes and any supplementary material (duplicated material, press clippings, etc) which they may gather as they proceed; help with additional study aids (which are dealt with elsewhere in this book) should also be given. It is always well to remember that adult students are often not familiar with or have long forgotten about elementary aids to study. A systematic card index is often useful for them to build up a reference system at home, and guidance on filing and indexing references may be helpful. When students have gained a place at Ruskin or Coleg Harlech they often ask for advice which one would have supposed they would have previously acquired from their teacher. The most obvious points frequently need spelling out, and encouragement from the teacher will ensure that the student does not feel embarrassment in asking for elementary advice. Although one always wants more material to hand than there is time to use, it is well to beware of attempting too much. It is surprising how short a time the two-hour session proves to be, particularly when student participation is part of the schedule.

Feedback: Records, Reports

Feedback checks are necessary throughout the course and preferably during each meeting. It is important that this should be done for each course if there is to be measured progress. The criteria are so dependent on subject matter and the educational aims and values that no detailed statement can be made. Only when these are known can the teacher devise his own system.

It is practically impossible to keep in mind accurately the progress of individual students, hence it is important to keep some record and assessment of each one. There appears to be some reluctance to do this, perhaps because of an inability to escape from thinking in terms of school reports and because of the tendency to classify students in examination terms. Yet it is difficult to see how systematic student follow-up can be maintained without some system of records; some form of card index is probably the most useful. Noting the particular difficulties and problems which students face is the only way to help them constructively over a long period. One only needs to reflect on the extent to which this is common practice amongst social workers, probation officers, doctors and school teachers. Clearly some background of awareness of psychological aspects and of types of people and temperaments will help, not only in recording, but in bringing about greater awareness of the learning methods appropriate for each individual. The use of a teacher's class diary to record the progress of class discussions and the follow-up required for the next meeting can be strongly recommended. This progress report will help the teacher to be aware of the comprehension level. It is also advisable to remember to discuss the syllabus for the next session with the students toward the end of the course.

FURTHER READING

Corfield, A. *How to Be A Student* (1968)
Highet, G. *The Art of Teaching* (1951)
Hoggart, R. *Teaching Literature* (1963)
Kidd, J. R. *How Adults Learn* (New York 1959)
Lawton, D. *Social Class, Language and Education* (1963)
Maddox, H. *How To Study* (1963)
Richmond, W. K. *The Teaching Revolution* (1967)
Rogers, J. (ed). *Teaching on Equal Terms* (1969)
Trenaman, J. M. *Communication and Comprehension* (1967)

5 The Use of the Talk in Adult Classes

Derek Legge

This chapter is concerned with the type of teaching technique in which one person presents a spoken discourse on a particular subject. As is common in adult education, the word 'talk' is thus used loosely to include a number of apparently different techniques, although essentially the differences are in manner or form of presentation rather than in the teaching situation they establish. Perhaps the most usual form is the one-hour lecture, traditional in some types of adult classes and still widely used in them as well as in universities and meetings of many voluntary organisations. The talk, however, may be given by a student or by a visitor to the class and may be only five or ten minutes in duration. Similarly, much of what follows is applicable to the interview, the symposium and the 'brains trust' type of panel presentation also used in some adult classes, as well as to the address given to a large adult conference or a sermon to an adult congregation. These are in fact only variants of the talk or lecture technique and the nature of the process remains the same; the learners are relatively passive participants, required only to listen while one or more people are actively trying to produce educational change by talking to or at them. Attention in what follows is largely focused on the uninterrupted talk given by a teacher in an average sized adult class, but the comments about the use and effectiveness of this in promoting adult learning have a wider context.

GENERAL FACTORS ON WHICH EFFECTIVENESS DEPENDS

Before turning to the particular features of this technique it is worth while to review the factors which condition the effectiveness of all methods in adult classes and which should indeed determine their choice by the teacher. Although a counsel of perfection, it can be urged that a teacher, before taking a class, should try to answer a question framed somewhat as follows: 'given this particular group of students meeting under these circumstances at this point in time, in this environment, with this type of subject matter and me, what are the desirable educational objectives and how best can I help students achieve them?' The choice of techniques and methods indicated in the final part of the question is clearly dependent on the earlier part, ie upon factors such as the following.

The Types of Student

Failure to select methods appropriate to the real needs and interests of the students as well as to their age, sex, educational and social background etc, will weaken the educational achievement. Moreover, student attitudes to the method are of considerable importance in determining success or failure. If the students are hostile to it, if, for example, they 'dislike talks' of any kind, they will usually erect effective emotional barriers to the learning it seeks to produce. These attitudes are often conditioned by earlier experiences and by the habits of the group, and if an emotional climate favourable to learning is to be achieved they must be modified, but they can be modified only gradually. For a time, therefore, a teacher may have to use a method which the students have come to accept and indeed favour. The writer remembers a class in which the students demanded that he should return for a time to the one-hour uninterrupted lecture which they had found pleasurable with previous teachers, even though in his view other methods would have been preferable. Only after some months did they cease to resist the alternative methods. Similarly, it has to be remembered that if any technique is to be effective students must be familiar with it and must know something of what is required. As will be suggested later, discussion techniques often fail until the students have learnt something of the discipline required of participants in a discussion, and similarly talks may fail in adult educational classes where there are students who are not accustomed to listening to talks. For them a talk of more than a few minutes is often of little value as an aid to learning, although at a later stage, when they have had more practice in listening rather than just hearing, they may find talks becoming increasingly helpful.

The Circumstances of the Class

Obviously the size of the group is an important factor, although too often a talk is regarded as the only way of teaching large classes. The suitability of time and place and, of course, the availability of facilities and resources are also determinants. If a class meets after a period in which the students have been relatively passive, perhaps after a day of talks, then not much learning is likely to result from a continuation of the same situation. The type of seating, the availability of power points, the adequacy of heating or ventilation, and other physical factors, must be taken into account if the teaching is to be effective. Anyone who has given an uninterrupted talk in an ice-cold room, or in a stuffy over-heated room, or even in one with extremely comfortable armchairs knows the futility of the enterprise. With ingenuity a teacher can sometimes modify the environment in which he has to work, but it is not a factor to be disregarded.

The Type of Subject
Methods need to be modified to meet the different requirements of mainly factual subject-matter and of controversial, more speculative matter. Where there are various interpretations or tenable alternative theories it is usually more helpful to use techniques designed to get maximum student participation than to employ didactic methods such as the uninterrupted talk, especially if the adult students are deeply involved emotionally in the subject, as is apparent in some classes on politics or religion. Discussion methods, on the other hand, are not of much value with subjects which, at any rate at the level of the class, are concerned with undisputed facts, while for many craft subjects practical work under guidance is clearly more helpful than any other method. One learns how to drive a car or to cook essentially by trying to use the skills required. It is also clear that there are differences between subject matter which is relatively familiar to the class members and matter which is completely new to them. New material may require techniques which allow plenty of time for adjustment and slow assimilation, whereas care has to be taken with familiar material to avoid methods which seem to produce too much or too slow a repetition. The talk which, in a revision lesson, attempts to repeat what has been said earlier in a course often produces student boredom and feelings of a waste of time. Other methods, such as the quiz, may in some subjects be more helpful to the students. On the other hand, if very new information is not available in any other way, then oral transmission by a speaker would seem to be the only possible method, although if there is a little forethought the products of even very recent research can usually be presented in dupli-cated form.

The Educational Purposes
Often these will vary from meeting to meeting and require a diversity of methods. The educational objectives may differ from student to student and a sequence of different techniques may have to be used, each of which is designed to help some members but not the whole group. This is not the place to discuss the question of how the objective is

determined—by the teacher, by the students or by some outside body such as an institution or examining board—but it cannot be emphasised too much that clarity of purpose is of great importance. There is a good range of purposes from which to choose. It is often asserted that the talk is valuable as a way of imparting information, and indeed that only this method can 'cover the syllabus in the time available'. What are not mentioned so frequently are the queries about the amount of information likely to be imparted in a given time, about the type of information most suitable, about possible alternative methods and about the length of time for which the information is to be retained. There is some evidence, for example, which suggests that the talk may be a suitable way of helping students with short-period retention of information in order to carry out a task which they are unlikely to repeat. Numerous other purposes can be considered. It is said that the talk can be used to stimulate interest, enthusiasm or action, that it can demonstrate arguments, points of view or propositions, or even how the mind of the speaker works, and that it can clarify the understanding of information which has already been assimilated. Few would suggest that it has any merit in modifying attitudes, values or behaviour patterns, although in practice many seem to use it in an attempt to reach these objectives, like the old preacher who attributed his supposed success in reforming the morals of his community to his repeated sermons.

The Teacher's Own Characteristics and Skills

Although most teachers can learn to be reasonably skilful in using a wide range of techniques, it seems clear that each tends to show special aptitudes for certain methods. Some are particularly good at lecturing, while others have a flair for methods requiring more student participation. Although outside the range of this chapter, it may be asked if more use might be made in adult classes of team teaching in which various teachers are specialists in particular methods rather than in particular aspects of the subject. The danger, of course, is that an individual teacher may reject without trial methods which do not fall within the particular rut he has created; the self-imposed limitation in the range of teaching methods which is an ever present temptation to all educators. What is here suggested is that teachers should try to assess their own skills in the use of teaching techniques and select their methods so that they make the maximum use of those in which they have the greatest competence, perhaps because temperamentally they find them the most agreeable.

THE CASE FOR THE USE OF THE TALK

Enough has been said in the preceding paragraphs to indicate the dangers of sweeping generalisations about the suitability or otherwise of the talk as a teaching technique. It has been subject to passionate denunciation or defence, but the contenders have relied usually on very subjective evaluation and exaggerated one-sided arguments. In fact, like all educational techniques, the talk has strengths and weaknesses, and it is worth looking at both in as dispassionate a manner as possible, especially as the number of educational talks has certainly not diminished in recent years and has probably shown a very considerable increase.[1] Perhaps one of the most important reasons for this continued popularity is the ease and economy with which the talk can be mounted. In itself the technique does not require elaborate equipment or accommodation, and indeed it can be used virtually anywhere, in the open air as well as inside, in all types of climate and for all sizes of group. On the whole it appears as an economic use of manpower, one person trying to help the learning of many people at the same time. Essentially, too, it has been a normal form of human communication since man learned to use language, and it therefore tends not to produce the emotional fears created when techniques and methods are used which are unfamiliar to the student. This familiarity and ease are not unimportant when assessing the contribution of a talk to the amount of learning in an adult class. As is suggested above, some students may indeed demand talks as the standard method to which they have grown accustomed and from which they believe they can obtain value and assistance.

In many subjects an organisational framework is required, and the talk has value in allowing for a systematic presentation. It gives reassurance to students who feel 'lost' and unable to 'see the wood for the trees', and also provides a general framework in which the student can see the coherence of the information and ideas with which he is confronted. In some subjects he may be helped in his learning by seeing the way in which the teacher marshals the subject content, especially perhaps if the subject is concerned with logical argument. In contrast, other types of technique requiring more student activity may often produce a confusion and lack of precision which increase the emotional learning problems of the student.

Of course, it may be said that this structure and order could be given more effectively in books. Ironically it is sometimes true that the really hopeless teacher, ie one who fails to communicate at all, drives the good student to go to the library to do the work for himself, achieving entirely satisfactory examination results. On the other hand, given the pressure of examinations and of students who find it difficult to learn by reading, there is a case for the talk as a substitute for a textbook. The talk, moreover, when competently given, does allow for the direct person-to-person contact in which the teacher's ideas and convictions, as well as information, can be conveyed by his manner, tone of voice, display of emotion and way of choosing words. A student may also be aided by the reactions of his fellow-listeners, and a good speaker will adjust his material as necessary to meet needs as they appear to develop. Flexibility is possible; the content can be expanded or condensed to suit the student audience and up-to-the-minute changes in information can be included. Critics of the talk often ignore its value in stimulating interest, in producing controversy and in giving inspiration, just as much as they forget the feedback from the student group in the form of facial expressions, gestures and movement. Great enthusiasm can be generated in a whole class by a speaker who is really interested in helping others to appreciate and understand his subject. To achieve this kind of value, however, requires a high degree of responsiveness and standard of performance.

POSSIBLE LIMITATIONS OF THE TALK

However great the possible visual feedback, it remains clear that the technique requires little active participation by the students and that this raises doubts about its value in helping the learning process. Learning requires student effort and activity and, despite the belief of some students, knowledge cannot be poured into human minds. There is indeed a kernel of truth in the often-quoted comment of the late Professor Joad that 'a lecture is the means whereby the contents of the lecturer's notebook are transferred to the notebooks of the students without passing through the minds of either'. However sensitive the speaker, the uninterrupted talk makes close contact with an audience difficult, if not impossible, and he cannot be sure what is being assimilated or rejected. He may be misled by an appearance of interest or by an industrious scribbling, and he may be tempted into a 'take it or leave it' approach, blaming the students for any failure to achieve educational objectives. Because of the degree of remoteness, little help is likely in the treatment of emotional blockages to learning, and indeed in large classes the particular needs of the individual are likely to be ignored because they are not openly apparent.

The danger of a mentally inactive process indicated by Joad is not, however, the major limitation in the use of the talk. What is more usual is great variation in the amount of assimilation caused by human inability to concentrate for more than a relatively short period. Some would assert that human beings cannot concentrate for more than four or five minutes, and certainly some of Trenaman's experiments suggested that after fifteen minutes most talks become ineffective.[2] What is clear from most tests is that there are considerable fluctuations in the degree of concentration by each listener, that there is no common audience pattern, ie class members concentrate at different periods so that some are most inattentive when others are listening intently, and that a particularly interesting statement by the speaker may actually deflect the listener's interest for the next five or ten minutes. The dilemma in fact is that without interest there will be no learning but that the more interesting the material the more likely it is that parts of a talk will not be heard at all, because the mind has been stimulated to wander along the path of interest. It is also true that there is a tendency to select what fits one's preconceived ideas about the subject, ie that often one only hears what one wants to hear. A former Director-General of the British Broadcasting Corporation has said that one of the surprising things about broadcasting is the fact that people hear what has not been broadcast, and this is equally applicable to the talks given in adult classes. When a class has been keenly interested in a talk, it is not unusual shortly afterwards to find an argument about what had been said, and if teachers can see the notebooks of their students they are often surprised by the inaccuracies in them.

This danger of distortion is increased by the need of the speaker to select his material for the talk. Inevitably he is tempted to over-emphasise for the sake of definition, to oversimplify in order to get clarity, and to eliminate qualifications. Indeed, without doing so he may produce confusion and bewilderment in the minds of the students, which in turn may cause emotional rejection of all the material. This sort of dilemma is inherent in the use of the uninterrupted talk, but it is also present when some other method is being used, notably in student reading of printed material. With the talk, however, it is particularly important, because unless there is a recording of the talk to which the student has easy access—not a usual condition in an adult class—there is no way in which a student can check the material or the accuracy of his memory.

Major limitations of the talk are thus essentially concerned with weaknesses in the contact between the speaker and the student, with relative failure to solve the emotional problems of learning and with general defects in communication. Tests have suggested that its value in promoting learning varies a great deal according to the type of student and perhaps particularly according to his level of intelligence and amount of previous education and knowledge. It would seem that those who are already knowledgeable, and those with above average education and intelligence gain most from talks[3], but further than this, that the value of a talk is linked to the attitude of the student which in turn reflects his personality.[4] When thinking about the use of the talk, therefore, a teacher has to recognise the generally haphazard nature of the method; for some students it may be very helpful, for others virtually useless.

MAKING THE TALK AS EFFECTIVE AS POSSIBLE

If, despite these limitations, the factors outlined in the first part of this chapter suggest that the talk is the appropriate technique, then clearly every effort should be made to make it as effective as possible. On the whole this means that attention should be given to the speaker's competence in the use of the method, ie his skill in delivery, and secondly to certain general factors related to the construction and framework of the talk.

Technical Competence

It is, of course, quite untrue to suggest that there is one correct way of delivering a talk; each teacher needs in fact to develop his own style. On the other hand a relatively small number of simple points, of basic essentials, apply to all talks.

In the first place there can be no communication unless the speaker is heard; this is so obvious that it is only worth mentioning because many adult educational groups still suffer from the inaudibility of speakers. With increasing age there is an increased likelihood of some deterioration in hearing as well as vision, and teachers should therefore give special attention to audibility when they have older classes. There is indeed no excuse for a failure to be heard. Most human beings have the necessary equipment to make them audible to large numbers without the aid of a microphone, and inaudibility is usually caused by indistinct pronunciation, particularly of consonants, by poor flexibility of lip and jaw muscles and by incorrect breathing. Breathing problems resulting in speech which lacks vigour ('throaty' speech), or in noisy gasps or jerky speech, are sometimes the result of the speaker's belief that he should breathe in some special way; but except when beset by colds or other infection most human beings need only to breathe naturally, relaxing their throat, shoulders and chest as much as possible. Otherwise audibility is a matter of practice in opening the mouth and in clear enunciation.

Secondly, speakers should cultivate those vocal qualities which tempt people to continue listening and make the communication as easy as possible for them. Most people become quickly tired of jerky, irregular speech, and in contrast respond well to reasonably fluent speech which has a good rhythm and is animated and alert. Likewise fatigue causes listeners to 'switch off' if a speaker talks too quickly. As St John Rumsey, a consultant speech therapist at Guy's Hospital wrote in 1949, 'If a thing is worth saying, it is worth saying slowly . . . slowly enough to be heard is good : to be so easily heard that you may be understood is better; to be so easily understood that what you say may be remembered is best of all'.[5] Sometimes audiences can be put off by over-slow speech, but most speakers would improve their effectiveness if they reduced their speed, either in the actual flow of words or in the flow of thoughts and of content. Adult students need time to digest what they hear, and the more unfamiliar the content the more time they need. Also, communication is kept open if speakers cultivate variety in their utterances. The monotone is a well-known method of producing sleep rather than listening, but it is also true that variations in pitch, in volume, in the speed of delivery, in the length and placing of pauses etc all help the students to listen without undue strain. Similarly the language used should be clear and intelligible to the particular audience. Though simplicity in words is a generalisation which is helpful in many classes, some subjects require familiarity with technical words; the important factor is that they must be fully understood by all members of the class.

Thirdly, communication by the spoken word is also made more effective by attention to visual aspects. Much of the meaning is often gained by watching the speaker's expression and behaviour. To improve the effectiveness of a talk, therefore, it is necessary to take up a position in which all the class members can see the speaker's face. This usually provides the answer to the question whether a teacher should sit or stand, and certainly it condemns those who talk only to the blackboard. The only other matter of general importance in visual terms is the need to avoid as many as possible of the mannerisms which distract, irritate or alienate an audience. It would be unrealistic to suggest that all mannerisms should be eliminated, but it is possible to reduce the number of those which break the thread of communication. The list is endless; classes have watched spellbound the teachers who perform balancing acts on chairs, as well as those who at regular intervals clean their glasses, wind their watches, tap with pencils or march like sentries to and fro. Most of these actions are unconscious and teachers need candid friends to point them out, but they can be mastered given some determination and effort. What has to be remembered is that some mannerisms distract some members of a class but leave the others untouched, and that new visual peculiarities are always likely to appear. The price of success in this aspect of technique is certainly eternal vigilance—but this is fully justified in an adult class to which the students come already fatigued. Much the same applies to the spoken mannerisms, the 'ers and 'ums, the over-repeated word or phrase or the standardised opening or ending to sentences. If the student is led to give attention to the mannerisms rather than to the content of what is being said, little learning will take place.

From what has been said it will have become clear that there is little use for a talk read from a full script. This has many disadvantages in interrupting the close contact with an audience and in preventing adaptation, while in terms of technique it often has a bad effect on the speed of delivery, the use of pauses and general variations. Often the script produces an irresistible attraction for the speaker's eyes, even for the whole of his face as he bends over it, and the script is frequently produced in a written rather than a spoken style. Those who use the talk, therefore, are recommended to speak from notes, which may be in any form intelligible to the speaker but which allow him at a glance to regain his thread if he has been diverted from it. Notes can also help him keep a watch on the time.

Some General Factors

Notes imply planning, and there is little doubt that the clarity with which a talk is constructed is often one of the major factors which determine its value to the adult student. He needs to feel at one with the speaker in the sense that he knows where the talk is leading. In talks designed to convey factual information it is often helpful for the structure to be fully known to students at the beginning. In others, planned perhaps to give inspiration or enthusiasm, this will not be quite so necessary, but all talks should provide students with the maximum reassurance that they will not get lost, that they can follow the speaker with ease. For this reason, as well as for others, it is often helpful to provide points at which the talk is summarised in its various stages as well as in the conclusion.

A common fault is to attempt to communicate too much too quickly, in too complicated a way. Sometimes, indeed, a teacher of an adult class seems determined to include all he knows in order to satisfy his own conscience or to meet the possible objections of imaginary critics. Class members need to be extended and led forward, but this is not achieved by making them mystified and dissatisfied, unable to assimilate the mass of material flung at them. In most classes a talk should have only a small number of points, all well illustrated either visually or verbally; though the exact number of points will vary according to the nature of the subject and the types of student, the human mind is unable to assimilate material at a very rapid rate. As emphasised earlier in this chapter, a teacher must assess his class, decide what are the common needs of its members, and then work out how best he can attempt to fulfil those needs. In many talks he will be led to a drastic reduction in the amount he will include.

SOME VARIATIONS OF METHOD WHICH INCLUDE THE TALK

A review of the types of limitation listed earlier quickly suggests a number of modifications which are likely to improve the results achieved by the talk. The creation of opportunities for interruption is an obvious partial answer to the problems created by lack of participation. These can occur at planned intervals during the talk, and they may take the form of questions from class members to the speaker or vice versa, or of comments which in turn may lead to a period of discussion before the talk is resumed. Interruptions may also be more spontaneous, breaking into the monologue at any point, but if this is desired an adult class has to be encouraged by the teacher and an informality of relationships achieved; until interruption is accepted as a normal procedure it is unlikely that most students will attempt it. Students fear a rebuff, and on occasion will complain that interruptions break the thread of the discourse and their own understanding of the plan of the talk. As with all methods, a favourable attitude among the students is required before it can be effective. On the other hand the development of a mixed method of questions and discussion added to the talk seems to pay a good dividend once it is established.

A talk may follow a text and be essentially a commentary on it. Similarly, duplicated notes may be used in place of a text; these may be distributed in advance in the hope that they will be read before the talk, or they may be given out at the beginning of the meeting, in which case time must be given for their perusal. Audio-visual aids are invaluable both for their stimulus to interest and memory and for their help in maintaining good concentration, and their use is discussed elsewhere. As always, however, their value depends on careful planning and the selection of what is appropriate for the particular group at the particular time.

Present evidence therefore suggests that there is a place both for the uninterrupted talk and for the talk assisted by other techniques. Its value, however, is determined very much by the views and attitudes of the students, by the nature of the educational objective, by the clarity with which this is thought out by the teacher and by the quality of the speaker's use of the technique. Of these, the educational objective is probably of supreme importance.

NOTES

1 Statistics are hard to produce, but one example of increased use is in the development of the major women's organisations in Britain. In the Women's Institutes and Townswomen's Guilds alone, it is estimated that there are now not less than 25,000 educational talks *each month*.
2 Carried out in the 1950s, these were concerned with sound radio.
3 See Vernon, P. E., *An investigation into the Intelligibility of Educational Broadcasts* (1950)
4 See particularly Beach L. R., 'Sociability and Academic Achievement In Various Types of Learning Situations', *Journal of Educational Psychology*, 51 (1960), 208-12
5 *Times Educational Supplement*. 28 October 1949.

FURTHER READING

For evaluation the most important recent work is McLeish, J. *The Lecture Method, Cambridge Monograph on Teaching Methods, No 1* (Cambridge 1968)

See also Cooper, B. and Foy, J. M. 'Evaluating the Effectiveness of Lectures', *Universities Quarterly,* 21 (1967), 182-5

Trenaman, J. *The Length of a Talk. Report on an Enquiry into the Optimum Length of an Informative Broadcast Talk for the Adult Student Type of Listener* (1951)

For technique see Clark, E. K. and E. B. *The Art of Lecturing* (Cambridge 1959)

For general comments on the use of the talk see Cleugh, M. F. *Educating Older People* (1962), Ch 3

Highet, G. *The Art of Teaching* (1951)

Peterson, A. D. C. *Technique of Teaching,* vol 3 (Oxford 1965)

6 Practical Training and Individual Tuition
Derek Legge

THE IMPORTANCE OF ACTIVE PARTICIPATION

The case for student involvement and participation is simple. Learning is an active process and there is no known method of merely pouring knowledge into a student's mind. All that a teacher can do is to bring the student into contact with educational material (facts, skills, ideas, attitudes, beliefs, etc) and, by making it as attractive as possible, to help him to assimilate it. The assimilation—the modification which we call learning—has to come from within, however, and little will happen unless the student makes an effort. Good progress, therefore, demands that the student be involved in active participation. In some subjects this is often seen to be obvious by the student, however much he may be tempted to move the burden to the teacher. Thus in craftwork students generally recognise that they will not make much headway unless they try to perform the required skills, and similarly people are aware of the need to do language exercises or to practise the steps in a dancing class. Even so, it is still possible to find the student in a dressmaking class who persistently waits for the teacher to do the cutting out for her, and the member of a language class who seems to believe that just being present will somehow bestow the power to speak or write the language fluently within a short time. In more theoretical subjects it seems even more true that some students believe that the teacher can fulfil all their expectations without any effort by them. This can be seen in both technical education and in liberal study classes when students declare that the teacher 'must cover the syllabus' as laid down by an examining body, or that he must provide them with all the information they want, preferably by a lesson-long monologue.

As this attitude is still commonly met among adult students and even among teachers of adult classes, it is worth looking more fully at the way in which active participation can help to solve some of the problems of adult learning. The major obstacle to learning faced by adults is the development of emotional blockages which are often caused by their own supposed lack of ability, or by fears about the reactions of their friends and associates, or by the imagined threat presented by new information and ideas. If the student remains a relatively passive listener or watcher he tends to be defensive and to reject entirely material which he finds disquieting. He may indeed build a still greater fear barrier. If, however, he is led into active involvement he frequently finds that his fears are insubstantial and unreal and he therefore becomes more willing to consider and to assimilate the material. Finding himself actually achieving something of which he did not think himself capable gives him a great sense of satisfaction, and when he discovers that the new ideas or information are not so damaging as he had imagined, either to his own way of life or to his relations with his friends, he ceases to offer quite so rigid a resistance. Most teachers have seen examples of this in their own classes and it would appear to be valid for all types of subject. Thus the student who finds that he has come to understand a scientific theory, or the causes and results of a sequence of events in history, largely by his own hard work, experiences the same satisfaction as the student in a craft class who proudly exhibits the piece of pottery or the finished coat. In the same way the student in a good language class finds his emotional barriers are reduced when he speaks the language in front of his companions and finds that he is not the object of ridicule and isolation he had feared he would be. In some classes, perhaps particularly those in local history and social studies, student excitement at making a small addition to the existing stock of knowledge often releases unexpected abilities. From an increasing amount of evidence[1] it is clear that adults learn less easily through imitation and 'being told' than they do through active exploration of the subject matter. Only by this emphasis on self-reliance and independence can the adult student expose and hence reduce the learning difficulties he experiences.

PROBLEMS OF INVOLVEMENT

One difficulty often faced by teachers anxious to encourage participation is the hostility of the students to the idea as well as their reluctance to bestir themselves 'unnecessarily'. This hostility may be caused by the contradiction between the activity proposed and their memories of childhood experiences, by views of what being in a class should be like in terms of methods and the teacher's role, or by beliefs associated with older ideas about learning. A direct attack by the teacher on these ideas will often produce, not only the defiance indicated by Bruxner, but also a development of emotional tension which will in turn increase the blockages which participation seeks to reduce. Students may refuse directly to undertake practical exercises (as did the man who told the author that he had been in classes for seven years without doing any written work and that he was not going to start now), but more usually they find polite excuses why the exercises are not done. It is essential for a teacher to recognise that movement to a greater degree of student independence and activity will be slow in many groups of older adults brought up in a different and contrasting tradition. He can only take the students with him as quickly as they are willing to go. As they come to realise the value of involvement and activity they will accept it more and more easily, but attempts to force the pace are likely to lead to difficulty. As always, understanding of student views, patience and encouragement, together with the essential establishment of good relationships, are the keys to success.

In adult classes teachers should be able to appreciate the not infrequent student opinion that, as the teacher is being paid, he must demonstrate that he is earning his fee. It is not only in children's schools that there may be a feeling that 'we do the work and he earns the money'.[2] This type of resistance, however, usually disappears in adult classes as soon as students understand the process and feel that the teacher is sincerely trying to give of his best in helping them to learn. What is most difficult for some teachers is the fact that practical 'discovery' exercises and independent student learning take the teacher off his pedestal and make him in a real sense the servant rather than the master of the group. The teacher indeed may appear to be just incidental. It is tempting to be the 'dispenser of crumbs of wisdom' and teachers in their anxiety to help are all too frequently led to play too active a part. They may therefore have to teach themselves—by practice—the art of self-denial, or letting students pursue learning largely free from control, and of being a resource person to be called upon when needed.

THE CENTRAL PROBLEM: TRAINING IN SELF-RELIANCE

The greatest problem for most adult students, however, is that they have been trained inadequately, if at all, in self-reliant study and in methods of practical work. Frequently they do not know how to study independently or to undertake the practical exercises or other forms of participation suggested, and it is therefore necessary for teachers to provide the necessary training. Sometimes this can be a simple demonstration, followed by supervised activity which gradually develops into independent activity, as for example in an elementary cookery class, but in other groups a more elaborate form of training may be required. All types, however, need to be carefully planned by the teacher, who must think through the whole of the activity stage by stage. The various processes may seem obvious to the teacher but are often quite the reverse to the struggling student. As with written or printed instructions, students need to be familiar with the words and phrases used, with the types of equipment or books, and with the sequence of method or steps which will be helpful. Although teachers tend to omit the stages in the process by which they have learnt their subjects, they must make effort to see them again through student eyes. Bewilderment and uncertainty will not help the emotional learning problems of the adult student, and if he attempts the activity at all in this condition he may be led to develop faulty habits of work. In many cases, however, he will either give up the subject or part of it because it seems beyond him, or with a false optimism he may rush away in the wrong direction and face a total failure. The untrained student can easily view the work as being more simple than it really is and try out what he thinks are comfortable short cuts to knowledge. Sometimes, indeed, students are tempted to try to complete their study or work task without waiting for the necessary information or guidance from the teacher; the result is almost inevitably a great deal of dissatisfaction and discouragement. An example the author recently came across was that of a very inexperienced member of a dressmaking class who rushed ahead at home making buttonholes in a coat without waiting for demonstrations and supervised practice. Despite the efforts of the teacher at the next class meeting the result was the waste of some fairly expensive material and an emotionally upset student.

Older students are often reluctant to accept that they have made a mistake or even to recognise that it exists, even when, as in a craft class, there is visual proof of the error. Similarly they are often unwilling to reveal that they do not know how to proceed, especially if everyone else appears to have no need of explanation. One is sometimes tempted to call this a conspiracy of silence which may extend to every class member, but it is, of course, both a revealing indication of the sensitivity of the adult student and a very human defence against possible ridicule and belittlement. A student once said 'Surely every adult knows how to do this . . .'; yet neither he nor his fellow class members could demonstrate how. Every possible guidance and help is needed, and this implies both a very full explanation of how to do practical work suggested and an attempt to match the assignment to the student's available time and energy. If the student thinks that too much is suggested, often nothing is attempted, and if the amount of work is, in his mind, extremely vague, he is unlikely to begin something which he fears he cannot finish. 'Find out what you can about the history of your town' may be a suitable injunction for those who have had some training in methods of historical enquiry, but it is unlikely to be helpful to a beginners' class in local history. On the whole, in most subjects, it is desirable to suggest a series of clearly understood but limited assignments designed to build up confidence as well as knowledge and understanding without making exorbitant demands on the students' available time. 'A little and often' seems to be clearly the preferable basis for the encouragement of independent practical work, either by individuals or by groups.

This type of programmed approach is now becoming more widely used and is often encouraged by the publication of various types of 'teach yourself' books. In many classes the basic method of demonstration, supervised activity and then independent work followed by discussion of its quality and problems, can be adapted for use at almost any level. Although perhaps it seems particularly appropriate to craft subjects, physical and health education and language teaching, it can be applied to almost all subjects. At a simple level it can be applied to teaching how to mend a fuse or to disbud chrysanthemums but it should be noted that 'simple' is a value judgement not necessarily accepted by students. In art appreciation, a full description of the techniques of a particular artist may be followed by students attempting to do likewise in order to deepen their understanding, while in sociology classes groups may be led to construct their own enquiry questionnaires and carry out a survey. The variations are infinite but in all it is clear that it is essential

1 to ensure that the learner knows exactly what he is expected to do ;
2 to make sure that he is not attempting too much either in terms of his available time or of his present state of knowledge. Students need to be stretched but it is better to do this in easy stages ;
3 to allow him within these limits to plan as much of his own programme as possible and to proceed at his own speed. Confused and bewildered students will erect obstacles.

The necessity for student training in activity or self-education methods applies just as much to the two forms of study most commonly used in a wide range of subjects : reading and written exercises. Too often it is assumed that all students know how to use books for study purposes and that all a teacher needs to do is to advise them to 'read the instructions in this leaflet' or to 'read some of the following books'. If we are accustomed to using books ourselves, we often show little awareness of the kinds of problem our students face when asked to read a page of print. For most people reading a book means beginning at page one and proceeding steadily to the end; yet for study purposes it may be far preferable to use the index or contents page for selective reading, or to glean the required information or viewpoints from several books by 'dipping and skipping'. Students often do not appreciate that different types of books need different treatment, that some are better read rapidly, while others need sustained if fairly slow, steady reading, that some are for consultation only as reference works, while others provide background knowledge etc. Although many difficulties in reading are caused by failure to understand key words, not many students are accustomed to use dictionaries to check meanings. Every possible guidance must be given, and·it is often helpful to discuss with adult classes methods of reading for study purposes and to demonstrate the techniques most likely to be useful. Part of a class period can be given to supervised practice by the students, perhaps working in pairs, and if assignments are then suggested for completion during the following week the results should be checked at the beginning of the next meeting. Most of our adult population has left school without the skills which help students to obtain the maximum aid from the printed word, and to training in the actual use of books and pamphlets has to be added training in the use of libraries or book collections of any kind. All adult students should emerge from classes able to find their way to additional knowledge in the subject, but to reach this result teachers must provide very careful supervision as well as reading lists full of comment and annotation.

It is also true that few students have adequate knowledge of how to carry out or to present written exercises. 'Make notes on this chapter' (or radio talk, etc) is often much misunderstood and can result in the expenditure of a considerable amount of student time with little gain. Very few have been trained in the art of making notes, and if this is true of most members of a class a teacher can demonstrate, perhaps by a summary on the blackboard or overhead projector, how to select, structure and arrange the material. Some teachers use their own talks as examples, at first putting down very full notes on the blackboard and then reducing these, as the lessons progress, to main headings and sub-headings and finally just to main headings. Others have used model duplicated notes as a basis for class discussion of methods of note-taking. Adult students are often reluctant to admit that they do not know these methods and, though it requires tact and diplomacy, it is essential for a teacher to see the students' notes and preferably to discuss these individually. Similarly, if experiments or collections of material are being written up, or if students are being asked to make written reports on visits of enquiry, the method must be demonstrated and student work supervised until the teacher is sure that each student knows exactly what is required.

Written work of an essay or examination answer type is well known to be difficult for many adult students, even in liberal study classes, and it is clear that for many it is a very laborious process and one about which many students have little understanding. Although it is perhaps now unusual for a teacher to receive a long, unpunctuated and unparagraphed script without any discernible order, it is still easy to find examples which show that many students do not know how to collect information and ideas, select and organise what is relevant, and then plan the essay. In these circumstances the teacher has to decide if this type of formal written work is likely to be useful to his students and if the class meets for a long enough period to allow for effective training in the method. If he believes that both questions can be given an affirmative answer, he will often find that much individual treatment has to be given. This usually means a lot of ingenuity in adjusting the type of essay subject to meet the different interests and capacities of the students, and then a patient discussion of the way in which a satisfactory result can be achieved. When the written work has been produced, it is essential to provide very full and courteous comment, giving encouragement by indicating how the essay might be improved rather than destroying confidence by too ruthless a criticism. As with public speaking, beginners should not be subjected to over-dismal inquests, but the more practised a person becomes the more rigorous should be the criticism. A teacher may find himself writing more than the student, but this indication of belief in the worthwhileness of the exercise may be in itself most helpful to the student.

INDIVIDUAL TUITION

Private tuition has often been regarded as an ideal method of learning, and it is clear that it has many advantages. By its nature it requires a two-way contact with good student participation and it is virtually impossible for the student to be completely inactive without terminating the process altogether. He cannot feel neglected in favour of other students and he is able to proceed at a pace which he finds reasonably comfortable. The direct contact has the most important advantage that it provides the teacher with an immediate feedback and enables him to come to a close understanding of particular difficulties. Through it he can give help and encouragement at the point where they are most needed.

In the more usual part-time evening adult class it is difficult to provide an adequate service of individual tuition unless the number of class members is very small, a situation not usually permitted. When the group meets only once a week the teacher can attempt to give individual help by arriving early and departing late, so that those students who can do the same may have a few minutes of individual treatment. Sometimes occasions can be provided during a class meeting, either during a tea-break or by dealing with individual problems while the rest of the class is busily occupied with independent work. In many craft classes this is a common practice, and the teacher may spend much time moving from student to student and only occasionally carrying out class teaching or small group tuition. Language classes can be given exercises, either written or oral, while individuals receive special tuition from the teacher, and similar arrangements can be made for classes in technical subjects or liberal studies. In the latter there seems little reason why the traditional talk and questions or discussion should be regarded as valid on all occasions; training in self-education methods, combined with individual tuition, may be a valuable substitute. It is worth reflecting that many infant and junior schools set an example of high quality 'learning-through-doing' combined with individual tuition, even in large classes.

To obtain the maximum benefit from individual tuition, however, the relationship between teacher and student is of key importance. Unless there is a bond of trust and confidence the result can be disastrous. Personal attachments to provide individual training are used in many professions, including medicine, and if there is an antipathy between the individuals concerned, or if a student feels that he is being treated in an off-hand way, learning may be stultified. Sometimes, indeed, antagonism to the whole subject matter may develop. Those who use the method of individual tuition must believe it to be worth while and must be prepared to be extremely patient and understanding with difficult students as well as with students in difficulty. As a method it is very time-consuming, and the intensity of the contact can be exhausting to both the people concerned. It is useful to set an agreed time limit to each period of individual tuition and to vary the time between each period in accordance with student needs. Circumstances may not always permit this kind of flexibility, but it is important that students should not become too dependent upon one individual. To get really satisfactory adult learning self-reliance must be the aim, but, as indicated earlier, good tuition can show how it is to be achieved.

Individual tuition is often believed to be just a process of talking between teacher and student but it can mean that the student works alongside the teacher, observing what he does and copying his methods. In industry this has often been described as 'sitting by Nellie' and has been condemned as being inefficient. At its worst it can mean that the student merely gleans scraps of information without the teacher actively entering the process at all, and even when carried out rather more adequately it can result in false hypotheses by the student and in a distorted, highly selective imitation. The student may also unconsciously assimilate the likes and dislikes of the teacher, however undesirable these may be. To get the maximum benefit a teacher has to think out the objectives of the period of individual tuition, to plan how best the student can benefit, and to relate the content to his capacity. This requires as much, if not more, preparation than any other method. Thus in some subjects it may be of value to show how the teacher has gathered his evidence, interpreted it and arrived at his conclusions. This can be done by an oral exposition of the argument, the student being encouraged to note the characteristics of the process and its strength and weaknesses. If the content is outside the present grasp of the student, or if the step-by-step analysis is not carried out with skill, the result may be confusion or wrong interpretation. Similarly, unless the craft teacher accompanies his work with much oral exposition and carefully checks that the various stages are fully grasped, the student may benefit little. He may learn to carry out a series of actions mechanically but have no understanding.

A further possible weakness of individual tuition is the removal of those group pressures which can assist learning. Sometimes the group can reduce the speed of assimilation to that of the slowest member but it can also serve as a pace-setter and help to carry the individual student through those difficult periods when he feels that he is making little progress or perhaps none at all. If he works entirely alone he may tire quickly and become discouraged. With a teacher who is unsympathetic or apparently unaware of his problems he can feel isolated and incompetent. Praise from the teacher alone may not always reassure the person with fears about his own abilities. A group can add its encouragement and give much needed support, so that the student feels considerable satisfaction and significance as a member of it. Some would argue that there can be too much emphasis on the individual and that membership of a group provides an essential basis for easy assimilation. In a group, too, the student is likely to learn from his fellow members and may gain from them helpful understanding of the ways in which he can achieve the educational objectives. For some individuals one of the primary objectives may well be that of learning to live as a member of a group.

Obviously there is a place for both group learning and individual tuition in adult education. In both, however, the teacher may often find it useful to give help without seeming to do so, and to follow the advice given in the couplet

> Men must be taught as if you taught them not
> And things unknown proposed as things forgot.

NOTES

1 For example, Belbin, R. M. *The Discovery Method: An International Experiment in Retraining* (Paris 1969)
2 See Opie, I. and P. *The Lore and Language of School Children* (1959). The full quotation is
        God made the bees
        The bees make honey
        We do the work
        The teacher gets the money

FURTHER READING

Yorkshire Council for Further Education. *Handbook for Part-time Teachers,* 2nd edn (Leeds 1950)

Northern Advisory Council for Further Education. *Suggestions for part-time teachers of women's subjects,* 4th edn (Newcastle 1963)

Guinery, M. *How to Study* (1966)

Belbin, R. M. *The Discovery Method in Training* (1969)

Belbin, R. M. *The Discovery Method: an international experiment in retraining* (Paris 1969)

Parsons, D. 'Discovery Learning in Archaeology', *Adult Education,* 41 no 4 (1968), 241-9

Waller, R. D. *Methods at Holly Royde* (1965)

Jones, R. H. 'Reading in the Adult Class', *Adult Education,* 25 no 3 (1952), 197-204

7 Discussion Methods

Derek Legge

WHAT IS DISCUSSION?

Discussion has become a portmanteau word carrying a multitude of different meanings, and until the definition is made more precise any real comment on discussion methods is impossible. The most casual use of the word is to apply it to any kind of human exchange of words, so that any two people may 'discuss' a question at home or in a public house, while great assemblies as at the United Nations also 'discuss' world problems. In an adult class any period in which there are spoken contributions from group members thus becomes discussion, whatever the objective or type of contribution. Moreover, because in recent decades the word has had extremely favourable overtones, it has been used to cloak situations in which there is little, if any, exchange of words between people. Thus, just as a person may discuss things with himself, so a teacher may declare that he has discussed a problem, even though in fact he has given an uninterrupted talk. Writers, too, discuss matters in their books without any sort of dialogue. Even when there is an exchange of words, the so-called discussion may be merely a battle undertaken from entrenched and unchanging positions.

In moving towards a definition, it is sometimes useful to begin with negative aspects and to distinguish discussion from those activities, processes or techniques with which it is so often confused. Thus a debate in which people are concerned with making points against each other in order to destroy the views of rivals is not discussion. Real discussion is not a process in which people seek the intellectual liquidation of their opponents. Neither is it the somewhat degenerate form of debate in which members of a class make a series of separate speeches, often in an established 'pecking' order and repetitive of earlier speeches, but quite unrelated to each other. This kind of ritual, seen all too often in the 'discussion period' of old-established adult classes, was once described as 'an athletic contest of closed mind with closed mind', and is not unknown in the discussions of larger assemblies. Also to be distinguished from true discussion are the various types of question and answer period, whether they are basically questions from the students to the teacher or vice versa, or a mixture of quiz methods conducted independently of the teacher. They may be valuable techniques for use in adult classes, and indeed, like debates, are considered later in this chapter, but strictly they are not discussion.

The important distinguishing characteristics of discussion lie in its purposes and in the manner in which the activity is carried out. Thus the word describes not any group of human beings talking together, but a group seeking to put together their knowledge, ideas and opinions about one subject in a co-operative endeavour to learn from each other. Instead of the destructive rivalry of a debate, a discussion seeks to be constructive, to encourage members to speculate freely, to withdraw or amend earlier statements and to make adjustments to their opinions without fear of loss of status. In a real discussion people try to listen to each other, to learn from each other, and by working together to reach a little nearer to the truth or to the solution of the problem or to whatever other educational objective they have in mind.

THE VALUES AND WEAKNESSES OF DISCUSSION

One of the merits of discussion defined in this way is the frank recognition that usually people already possess information, feelings, interests and beliefs which profoundly influence the learning process. As an educational method, in fact, its importance lies in the way in which it impels class members to participate instead of being passive hearers. As suggested in Chapter 6, involvement tends to release some of the emotional blockages to assimilation. In particular it seems to be more helpful than other methods in enabling the student to modify attitudes and opinions, because it encourages him to examine them in an atmosphere from which as much threat as possible has been removed. As the method carries the implication that he does not need to be defensive, it becomes easier for him to minimise those fears and frustrations which stand in the way of satisfactory learning. If in any subject a student meets an idea or a technique or an attitude which he fears as a threat to his self-respect and competence because it contradicts his earlier way of life, then he is likely to offer a total resistance to it if presented in a talk; in a discussion, however, he may take reassurance from the readjustments being made by his fellow students and in a real sense he may 'talk out' his fears.

In a discussion people react more fully to the subject material confronting them because they have to think and formulate views about it, then state those views and then listen to the views of others. Class members are led to see that they have overlooked many aspects of the subject, that everyone has blind spots and that in order to arrive at a mature judgement they have to take into account many shades of opinion and meaning. They should also scrutinise the facts and reasoning of the teacher, who in the discussion situation is taken off his pedestal and drawn into a more equal relationship with students, at least in terms of the subject material. This more intensive contact with the subject in a permissive situation tends to produce more durable learning.

Stimulus to interest and understanding is the result of good discussion, although of course other methods may achieve the same end. Evening classes sometimes appear to gain a new life by the use of the method as adults shake off their fatigue at least for the period of the discussion. Most human beings learn better in a social context, as members of a group rather than as isolated persons, and the interplay of minds which takes place in discussion often sparks off new ideas, new trains of thought and new understanding. In a discussion, members of the group mutually reinforce the learning which is taking place, acceptance by the group as a whole making acceptance by the individual much easier. Indeed, because in the course of the conversation he becomes aware of the kind of learning approved by the group, he may be led to take active steps towards understanding and perfecting the modification in knowledge, activity or outlook which is desired. Sometimes these steps take the form of practice in self-expression, as a result of which the student develops powers he had not thought possible, and this in turn gives an increased self-confidence which improves his ability to learn, as well as having a marked effect on his general way of life. Many leaders in community life, in government, in the trade union movement and elsewhere have paid tribute to the process of self-development which for them took place in evening-class discussions. Almost any teacher of classes meeting for lengthy periods can quote examples of the sense of achievement and significance resulting from successful participation in discussion and of the beneficial effect this had on learning.

For the teacher there are obvious benefits to be obtained from discussion periods. Through them he can get a much closer knowledge of his students and of their problems; he can find out how much or how little has been assimilated through other methods, and often he can correct distortions and misunderstanding; he can use them to gain the sort of feedback which will help him plan the next part of the class programme and, in general, discussion periods help him in the development of the greater degree of social coherence likely to help assimilation. This contribution to good relationships is perhaps one of the greatest potential values of discussion, but it would be inaccurate to suggest that it happens automatically.

Discussion, in fact, is not the supreme answer to all the problems of the adult educator, despite some of the extravagant claims made for it. The list of virtues makes assumptions about the student group which are not always valid. Sometimes students have no previous knowledge of the subject matter and, if so, it is futile to expect them to learn from each other by trying to pool their non-existent facts and ideas. Satisfactory discussion cannot take place in a vacuum. Similarly, if the class members are inarticulate, with little power of oral self-expression, discussion can be a dreary, rather soul-destroying and on the whole profitless method to attempt. The only benefit likely to accrue is a slow improvement in oral communication, which may make for more rapid learning at a later stage, but a teacher has to assess what he can achieve in the time available and whether more could not be achieved by other methods. In general terms discussion, by its inherent nature, tends to be time-consuming and slow in the achievement of educational objectives, and it can be questioned whether the argument that 'what is learned is learned better' really atones for this at all times.

There are other weaknesses. The easy verbal exchange of facts and ideas is unlikely to be the best way of learning practical activities or indeed any subject which, at the level of the class, is composed of uncontroversial facts. Few would find discussion a very helpful way of learning craft work, how to cook, or how to drive a car. There may be a place for a limited use of discussion to examine driving problems, but most of the learning is likely to be better achieved by other methods. Discussion is most appropriate to those subjects concerned with controversial issues about which there are different but equally tenable opinions. An acknowledged fact cannot be discussed as such, and at the levels normal in adult classes discussion attempted in the factual areas of mathematics and the sciences can be largely a waste of time. Students indeed may assert that discussion methods have failed to achieve anything, even in classes concerned with controversial subject matter. Although this is usually a faulty subjective impression, it is worth noting that sometimes in a well-established class the students have already contributed so much of their knowledge and views that nothing new is being added. Like all other methods, discussion has to be used with discretion, after an assessment of all the circumstances.

Most of the weaknesses of discussion as an aid to learning, however, result from the failure of the teacher to use the method with skill and the failure of the students to take on the roles of good discussion group members. Usually lack of knowledge of what is required is the basic cause, but occasionally there may be a deliberate misuse of the method by either teacher or students. Thus a teacher with a group of students wanting authoritative guidance may be tempted to use discussion as a way of leading them to his own views, a process which is really one of manipulation, and similarly some articulate students may use the discussion as a vehicle for the conversion of others to their own beliefs, the classroom becoming a platform with a relatively captive audience. A more thorough knowledge of discussion techniques may give some protection agains misuse and will certainly assist the teacher trying to get the maximum benefit from the method.

TECHNIQUES OF DISCUSSION LEADERSHIP

Teachers using discussion methods often appear to imagine that they must be active throughout the discussion, whereas in fact they should be relatively silent, taking part only when they see ways of improving the effectiveness of the proceedings. In an ideal discussion there would be no need for leadership. All members would talk together freely and easily, without tensions or inhibitions; all would keep to the point, be constructive and intelligible to everyone else and would share out the time, neither monopolising it nor refusing to make a contribution; in the relaxed informal atmosphere all would tolerate differences of opinion and feel free to admit errors and mistakes and to accept criticism; and at the end of the discussion they would feel that they had achieved the desired objectives.

This is an unattainable ideal, but it points the way to the main tasks of a discussion leader. No human group is ever completely free from tension, but the leader has to try to keep the emotional tone as relaxed and permissive as possible. And secondly, because people tend to wander from the subject, to be unintelligible to others, to talk too much or too little etc, he has to try to develop good discussion behaviour in the members. Teachers have to recognise that in some adult classes the discussion will begin by being a long way from the ideal, and that even in classes which have reached a good standard of discussion there is always the danger of a class meeting in which almost everything can go wrong.

The Emotional Climate
Though ideally people talk freely, in reality the ease of conversation is reduced by tension, friction, feelings of inequality, doubts and resentments. Some general methods for the improvement of relationships have been discussed in Chapter 3, where it was noted that the physical setting can be of considerable importance in producing a more relaxed atmos-

phere. People will not converse freely if they are too hot or too cold, or if they feel uncomfortable because of the size of the room or its association with unpleasant experiences. Some adults feel inhibited in schoolrooms, churches or managerial premises in industry, but others have different emotional reactions. Part of the leader's task is to find a setting which helps his group to feel at ease, and if he has no choice over the type of accommodation he must modify what he has got until it is as helpful as possible. A simple example is a rearrangement of the seating. People talk more easily if they can see each other's faces, and a circle is by far the best formation for the group and its leader. If the seating is fixed or unsuitable in other ways, a leader should seek the arrangement of class members which allows each person the chance to see the greatest number of his fellows. Similarly the provision of cups of tea or other suitable drinks may help people to relax.

Perhaps the most important contribution a teacher can make to the emotional environment, however, is his own approach. By becoming sensitive to the views and circumstances of each member, he can try to make everyone feel that they are of importance and can try to minimise the inevitable inequalities of status and background. By his own good humour, by patience, courtesy and tact, and by cheerful enthusiasm he can ease the frictions and keep fears and antagonisms to the minimum. To make the conversation effective he has to secure a real equality of status within the group, at any rate for the period of meeting, and he can help this by setting an example, helping the group to achieve its objectives but not dominating it or allowing any member to do so. Trying to get class members to feel free and equal, especially when they may not want to be, is a delicate process dependent often on split-second decisions; the teacher therefore should not be unduly worried by failures, as he will merely increase them by introducing his own tensions. A practical measure which he can take in most classes is to provide opportunities for introductions and for contact between class members. People guard their conversation and act defensively if they feel that they are among strangers, and with a little planning and forethought a leader can get them to know each other fairly quickly. Some teachers in fact devote much of the first class meeting of the session to this process and regard it as time well spent.

Good Discussion Behaviour

Faced with many manuals laying down in detail what he should do, a discussion leader should realise that discussion is a process of human interaction capable of infinite variations. Slavish attempts to follow a set of instructions will not really help, and indeed by their rigidity they may produce unfortunate tensions within the group. Leaders should therefore keep in mind the characteristics of the ideal discussion, but should examine suggested techniques in a commonsense way, asking if they will in fact help the particular group with which they are concerned. In this connection it may be useful to look at the three main aspects of the technique. These can be listed as follows. (1) getting the discussion started, (2) keeping it fruitful (ie helpful to learning) when it has started, and (3) providing a satisfactory ending.

For some groups concerned with some subjects, the opening presents few problems. Just as many conversations begin without an artificially contrived opening, so in an adult class a brief sentence may be all that is required. Usually this happens when the topic is well known to the group, when perhaps the discussion is being used to deepen understanding of already familiar material, and certainly it needs good relationships and a relaxed atmosphere. Other subjects, however, may require a short introduction, both to provide some basic new information and to focus the mind of the group on the subject. It may also be necessary to provide an introduction which gives time for people to settle down and relax, especially if members have travelled long distances or have come straight from work. What has to be remembered is that the longer the introduction the less easy it is for the conversation to start; people sit back to listen and it requires more and more effort for them to change into active participants. A leader is therefore well advised to keep his introduction as brief as possible, provided that it achieves three objectives: to show the purpose, to focus attention on the topic and to give time for the group to settle down.

Sometimes the discussion does not start easily or may not start at all. Obviously the more a leader knows the members the more likely it is that he will be able to select suitable questions and topics which are of immediate interest to them, but the silence may be caused by the place or time or by some outside factor rather than by his faults of technique. Even so, he should ask himself if he has annoyed the group in any way, or if he has chosen a subject unsuited to the group at that point in time or if his introduction was badly phrased. A not uncommon error is failing to include enough controversial matter or putting in so much that there appears little left to be said by group members. Adults see no sense in mere repetition of the leader's remarks, and the omission of the most obvious points will often lead to a rapid opening in which they are put forward by several members. It is worth remembering, too, that people need time to put their thoughts into words; if there is a silence the leader should not rush in too quickly, as he may interrupt the process and tempt some members to leave all the talking to him. He has to try to sense whether the silence is caused by people having nothing to say or whether it is just a pause while they gather their

F

thoughts together. If the former, he may sometimes encourage the conversation by providing additional viewpoints or by asking for opinions on selected questions. In some circumstances, however, silence indicates the need for a change of method.

When the discussion has begun, the leader has the task of making it as helpful as possible to the group members. Sometimes it is asserted that he should insist on a planned framework, but in practice this advice seems much too rigid to be valid except in a small number of cases. Helpfulness can only be assessed in terms of objectives which may be long-term as well as short-term. Thus with a class in which the members are unused to discussion and are perhaps a little inarticulate or at least find it difficult to talk together, the first objective may be to encourage them to talk so that in the long run learning will be facilitated. In the early stages, however, the conversation may wander a great deal and may appear to be very unorganised. With a more experienced group, where perhaps the objectives are clarity of thought and analysis of argument, it is probably more helpful for the leader to become a chairman who tries to keep people to the point, to get them to be as concise as possible and to put forward only one topic at a time. It is vital indeed to keep flexibility so that the state of the group decides the degree to which the discussion is organised. In all discussions, however, it is helpful if the leader rephrases contributions from time to time, repeats the partly inaudible, interprets jargon and summarises the main points of a long and rambling statement. He can hope that by so doing he will gradually lead members to learn the rules of good discussion. In the meantime he has to set an example of good humour and efficiency.

One particular problem which faces all discussion leaders, and perhaps particularly the teacher using the discussion method, is the tendency of groups to make him the central figure, the dominant person to whom questions are directed and from whom every alternate contribution is expected. This changes the process into one of question and answer, for a discussion as defined implies that contributions should flow freely round all members of the group. Visually the difference may be portrayed as on the opposite page.

To avoid a change of method the leader has to discourage the development of questions directed personally to him (What do you think of . . .?) and indeed he is advised to throw back all questions to the group, especially questions of opinion, and to ask for answers from other members. Occasionally this rule may be broken if a brief piece of factual information, known only to the leader, will save the time of the group, but he should never rush to give an answer.

A second general problem is failure to share out the time in the way suggested by the ideal group. Most of us either talk too much or too

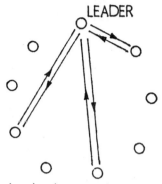

Leader dominated question
and answer pattern

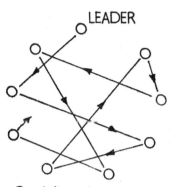

Good discussion pattern

little, and the amount of our contributions tends to vary from one meeting to the next. The leader, therefore, has a permanent task of trying to encourage quiet members to make some contribution and of attempting to restrain those who appear to want to monopolise the proceedings. This presents him with problems which may have many facets and indeed to which, at best, he can only hope for partial solutions. If he realises this, however, and attempts to assess each individual difficulty instead of applying a rule of thumb answer, he will usually find that there is a steady improvement in the quality of discussion.

Thus it is useless to imagine that all the quiet members are just shy and in need of the same treatment. Some may be shy in the sense that they have inferiority failings which cause them to be reluctant to speak in big groups, in large places or among people whom they imagine to be superior in knowledge or status. Others, however, are afraid of ridicule from their friends, and some have unreal fears of deficiencies in grammar or expression. For some silence has become an ingrained habit, perhaps the result of years of conditioning at home, in children's schools or in the community. Despite changes in the present century, it is still true that for many it seems safer not to speak. In contrast there are those who have no such inhibitions but fail to contribute because they are bored or convinced that discussion of the topic is futile.

Each needs separate treatment, although in general the creation of a friendly, informal atmosphere helps by reducing tensions and fears. The more the leader gets to know members and their interests, the more he can assess particular needs and what he might do about them. For some a carefully chosen remark on the subject matter may provoke a vocal comment, while for others an appeal for the special knowledge or experience which the leader knows to be in their possession may be the best way of getting them to talk. Direct questions, except to the bored, tend to be dangerous in that they may result in even more tongue-tied embarrassment; leaders must consider carefully the likely effect before they risk saying 'What do you think, Mr A?' Tactful encouragement when a small contribution has actually been made tends to lead to more contributions.

This often means restraining the over-talkative, who present a range of different problems. Sometimes they are just articulate and enthusiastic people who have never considered the role of a good group member. When informed about the importance of shared thinking they will often do their best to co-operate both by modifying their own behaviour and by encouraging quiet members. Others, however, know what their role should be but refuse to accept it. They may be aggressive types who think they know everything and refuse to learn, or people who like to hear the sound of their own voices, though they have little to contribute, or people with obsessions, or compulsive talkers, or deliberate obstructors or 'ramblers' who make long-winded, woolly statements which they cannot end. The list of types is a long one and there is no one answer other than a general one of patience and politeness. The leader has to try to understand each problem case and to find an individual solution. Sometimes he will find that talking about discussion methods is helpful, either in the group or privately with an individual. As with all teaching methods, it is generally worth while with adults to spend some time in making sure that they understand the nature of the process. Sometimes people will not respond and it may then be necessary either to use the pressure of the rest of the group or to act independently. Thus a group can be led to co-operate in imposing restraint, perhaps by analysis of the weaknesses of a long, repetitive contribution. Or the leader may have to insist on a contribution ending after a point has been made; if so he has to be sure that he has the general support of other members and that his action will not increase tensions. It cannot be emphasised too often that discussion technique is dependent on the social relationships existing between the people who use it.

Bringing a discussion to a satisfactory conclusion is also a matter of judgement. The leader has to decide the point of closure and bring the conversation to an end before the group is exhausted or bored and, in an adult class, before the educational profit has become minimal. In general it is much better to close when members are eager to continue the conversation than to allow it to grind slowly to silence. With some groups, especially those unaccustomed to the activity, this may mean a very short period of discussion; others which are well established may have a regular prearranged time limit based upon experience, but for all, discussion after one and a half or two hours tends to become educationally ineffective.

The type of ending required differs according to the purpose felt to be desirable. Sometimes it is possible to draw conclusions and to announce decisions, either final or tentative. If a class, for example, has been considering a project activity or writing up the results of a project, final decisions may be a suitable ending; on the other hand, if part of the object of the discussion has been to reveal the widespread ramifications of a topic, it may be preferable to indicate only the decisions which seem to have emerged by the time of closure and to suggest that these may be modified in the light of further information. In other subjects, any decision could be viewed as the attempt of the leader to mould opinions, and unless this is the purpose of the activity it is preferable for him merely to list the alternatives discussed and to stress the need for individual decisions. This would be true, for example, in a class which has been discussing the merits and demerits of alternative methods of central heating. In all discussions, however, it is essential for the leader to take enough time to ensure that the process is felt to have been of value to each individual. Usually this means that there will be a fair restatement of the main points which have been made—often class members are surprised by the amount of material revealed by such a review—and certainly a stress on the importance of the way in which they have helped each other by testing out the ideas, information, experiences, hopes and fears. Often, too, it is useful to suggest further aspects of the subject to be considered, perhaps in future class meetings, or lines of action which individual members may pursue.

Preparing for discussion

From what has been said it will have become clear that a teacher planning to use discussion methods needs to spend a good deal of time in preparation, perhaps almost more than for any other method. He has to consider not only the physical setting but also the emotional responses of each class member. He has to give forethought to his own style of leadership and to the ways in which he can more effectively find answers to the problems presented by 'awkward' students. Above all he has to think about the group interaction and how this will affect the learning process. To this wrestling with somewhat intangible issues he has to add thoughts about the subject, how best it can be introduced to the group, what aspects are likely to be most attractive to members, what the main discussable points are, what points of view on each are possible and how he will attempt to get a fair consideration for them. Since much of his leadership will consist of short comments put in after momentary decisions, the more he has thought through the discussion the more likely it is that his interventions will be helpful. In practical terms, the result of a long period of preparation may be only a single sheet listing the main aspects of the topic, possible alternative viewpoints or questions and possible illustrations, but such a period is essential if the maximum educational benefit is to be gained. Success in discussion is never complete but is well worth striving for.

VARIATIONS IN DISCUSSION METHOD

Discussion leadership in an adult class is usually assumed to be the prerogative of the teacher, but often it can be helpful to have a student as leader, provided that he has a knowledge of the required techniques. The teacher can then remain aloof, to be called upon when needed, or, more happily, can become an ordinary member of the group. For the latter to be successful his relationship with the group must be such that its members will accept his change of role without emotional stress. Many adult educational groups, of course, meet without a teacher present, as in the discussion group scheme organised in New South Wales since 1938 by the University of Sydney Department of Adult Education. There a box of books and other aids is sent to the group, which holds a regular fortnightly discussion and maintains correspondence contact with a distant teacher. Although this scheme was designed to meet a particular set of circumstances, the feature of student leadership in place of teacher dominance is a variation which might improve the learning process in many places.

Even with the most experienced group of people it becomes difficult to get good discussion if the number exceeds twenty, and usually smaller groups are more worth while. The group needs to be large enough to include the greatest possible variety of viewpoints and experience, yet small enough to allow each person to make his contribution with ease. In an average situation perhaps ten to fifteen is a good number, though some groups function best with seven or eight members and some with only four. Even a relatively small adult class of twelve may therefore find it helpful to divide into two or three discussion groups, the teacher perhaps sharing his time between them. With larger groups a division into units of four or five people who talk together and after a limited time report back to the whole class is also very fruitful. There is no need for a separate room for each unit; five or six separate discussions can take place without difficulty in the same classroom. During the period of reporting to the whole group a teacher can give considerable help by producing a summary, perhaps on a blackboard. The small units may take the same topics for discussion or may be allocated different aspects.

Various opening leads are possible besides the short talk by the discussion leader. Some classes have used short playlets or puppet shows to provide both the stimulus and relaxation of tension necessary to get an easy start to the conversation. Depending on the subject, suitable demonstrations, experiments or even competitions may achieve the same result, and other classes have used interviews, perhaps with a visitor, or informal debates or a period of question and answer. There is not just one way of leading a discussion and teachers should experiment with variations to find those most suitable to their students and to the purposes in mind.

THE USE OF DEBATES AND PANEL DISCUSSIONS

Although an activity different from discussion, a debate is so often confused with it that a few notes about usage and technique may be helpful. Despite the not infrequent condemnation, some use can be made of debates in adult classes, particularly to stimulate interest or to confront class members with sharply contrasting points of view or interpretations of the evidence. The overstatement which often takes place in a debate may lead students to be more resistant to overstatement elsewhere, especially if it is subjected to good-humoured analysis in a later class meeting. In many subjects too, it is useful for students to observe how an argument can be built up, how an emotional appeal may be made and how opposing argument may be twisted, especially if this is done within the set framework of a debate organised with an established order of proceedings and rules. The staged performance gives some emotional protection to the participants, while at the same time allowing them freedom to go beyond the boundaries of tolerance and courtesy normally acceptable in an adult class. Because it is a convention in a debate, people will often accept quite fierce denunciations without any real rise in tension. It is also true that participants have been known to modify their opinions because they have recognised the imperfection of their own arguments put forward in debate; though not openly admitted at the time or even later, the effect is evident as the class progresses.

The danger which teachers have to watch is the transformation of the staged performance into a personal argument which can severely damage relationships within the class and so impede learning. Debates, therefore, have to be carefully planned and introduced only when the class has already reached a good degree of friendliness and informality. In most classes the principal speakers—preferably two for the proposition and two against—may be drawn from the students, in which case it is desirable for the teacher to be the impartial chairman. The choice of proposition and of speakers, whether students or from outside, should be made well in advance and made known to the whole class. The same points also apply to the so-called panel discussion or brains trust in which a small group with a chairman consider a series of questions. The differences between a debate and a panel discussion are that in the latter a number of issues are considered instead of one proposition, that the tone is more informal and conversational without set speeches, and that a vote is not usually required, whereas in a debate there is a set order of speeches—proposer, opposer, seconder to the proposer, seconder to the opposer, and, in conclusion, the opposer followed by the proposer— in the panel discussion the more varied the order the better. Audience participation may be encouraged in either activity; in a debate after the first four speeches and in a panel discussion at any point when it seems likely to take place without a radical distortion of the process. Some- times most of the class would prefer to listen to the answers given by the panel rather than listen to one or two of their number conducting a per- sonal quiz. Some good use has been made of a divided session, in the first half of which a panel of outsiders answers written questions sent in advance by class members and then proceeds in the second half to ask questions of the class.

QUESTION AND ANSWER PERIODS

Often question and answer sessions are designed to reach objectives similar to discussion, especially in producing greater participation by class members. The most obvious type is that in which students ask the teacher for answers, either at the end of a talk or during it. With adults these questions may be put because the student is genuinely interested, or confused, or sometimes wanting to trap the teacher, but in all instances they should never be belittled. Seemingly foolish questions may be the fumbling attempts of a person unused to self-expression, and answers need always to be related to the emotional effect they have on the student.

For this reason questions from the teacher to the students need to be carefully phrased. A class may be led to accept a quiz as a legitimate learning activity, but until it does so questions to test the assimilation of factual information are not popular with most adults because they suggest an inferior student status. Sometimes, with caution, they can be used as a competitive game, but if so used the process must be clear to the students. On the whole a teacher's questions should either be those in which he genuinely wants factual information because he does not already have it—many adult students have specialist knowledge, if perhaps in only limited areas, of the subject they are studying—or those designed to provoke thought and reasoning. Leading questions are rarely helpful, and no question should be laboured to the point of boredom. Finally, a teacher may draw information and ideas from his students by a series of questions and lead them to formulate their own answers to problems and to build up their own knowledge into a composite whole. Often described as 'the Socratic method', this requires a high degree of skill and extensive preparation similar to that described for good discussion leadership.

FURTHER READING

Of the several pamphlets published on discussion leadership the following would seem to be the most useful:

Bureau of Current Affairs. *Discussion Method: The Purpose, Nature and Application of Group Discussion* (1950)
Lloyd, W. E. *How to Run Discussion Groups* (1944)
Spreadbury, K. S. *The Discussion Group Leader* (1944)
Adult Education Association of the USA. *How to Lead Discussions* (1955)

For comment on the value of the method see:

Burton, J. (ed). *Group Discussion in Education, Social and Working Life* (1955)
Ruddock, R. and Morris, J. F. 'Discussion in a WEA Class: A Quantitative Analysis', *Adult Education*, 28 no 3 (1955), 200-10
Radcliffe, A. H. 'Discussion Group Adventures', *Adult Education*, 27 no 3 (1954), 241

8 Role-Playing and Simulation Techniques

Arthur Stock

WHAT IS ROLE PLAYING?

R ole-playing is a comparative newcomer to the battery of techniques
now available to the adult educator. Although employed therapeutic-
ally by psychiatrists from the early years of this century, its use in
education has only recently been developed to the extent of its being
fully recognised as a valuable addition or alternative to other group
techniques.

That children take up roles within their own play groups was readily
recognised and commented upon by several nineteenth-century writers.
Thus Spencer[1], while propounding the dubious 'excess energy' theory
of play, nevertheless comments on the strong tendency to imitate. 'Play
is equally an artificial exercise of powers which in default of their natural
exercise become so ready to discharge that they relieve themselves by
simulated actions.'

While stressing the close relationship of art and play, Spencer antici-
pates Groos's 'theory of practice'[2] in relation to play. But a better
insight is offered into modern educational role-playing by Ebbinghaus[3].

> The boy who plays robber and police is not like an actor playing
> the role of a robber. He really is the robber so far as the advan-
> tages, the freedom and the power of the robber are concerned;
> and he enjoys these advantages, while the actor does not even think
> of them.

Modern investigations into the behaviour of individuals in group situations suggest that the child's instinctive adoption of a role when 'learning-
by-playing' is often repeated by the adult who is striving to learn about
the life around and within him. Parsons, Bales and Shils[4] describe the
process as it affects the person in a discussion group who 'gets on the
right track.'

> If such a person . . . . receives positive reactions from other
> members, he will be reinforced in his direction of movement, and
> will tend to keep on talking. . . . The member begins to build a

90

'specialised role'. In so far as the activity he performs is felt to be important in terms of the functional problems of the group, its goals and value-norms, the 'status' of the member will begin to rise.

More recent work[5] has identified a number of frequently adopted roles: 'the diplomat', 'the natural leader', 'the iconoclast', 'the ideas man', 'the comic' and even occasionally 'the scapegoat'.

Nevertheless the undoubted existence of role-playing as a phenomenon of unstructured play or social groups would not be sufficient of itself to warrant the building of a specifically constructed learning situation based on it. It is really the experience stemming from work in the clinical and social psychological field which has enabled adult educators to identify and codify this special technique.

Perhaps the most enthusiastic proponent of these ancestral forms of role-playing was Moreno.[6] His work in the refugee camps of central Europe following World War I, and his later work in the United States in the treatment of psychotic and neurotic disorders, gave rise to a 'socio-interactional' theory of personality; the self is seen as the sum total of various social and private roles which the individual plays in his interaction with others. The 'healthy' individual is the one who can recognise and comprehend his own roles and produce appropriate role responses. This, according to Moreno, was the skill essential in all human enterprise.

Applying this theory in a therapeutic way produced *psychodrama*. Here the main emphasis is on the individual and his specific problems. He is encouraged to act out a situation spontaneously, after being 'warmed-up' by the therapist. A number of trained performers assist by acting as 'auxiliary egos' to the patient. The role or roles which the subject plays will thus be a product of his own 'inner self', and the therapist is able 'to glimpse functional levels of intelligence and to detect behavioural efficiency in crisis situations'.

Moreno went on to deploy this method to attack 'social disease' in addition to the treatment of individual problems. He was concerned to deal with group problems such as ethnic or religious intolerance and cultural conflict. Thus the term *sociodrama* came to be used, where a particular group would improvise or act out a problem situation. Typical scenes would be a negro/white confrontation in an area where colour prejudice was strong.

In sociodrama the subject is not an individual, but a group. The characterisation tends to be in two-dimensional type roles rather than individuals, a 'Jim Crow' negro or a 'bring-back the birch' authoritarian.

Sociodrama and role-playing are often regarded as synonymous, but the essence of Moreno's method was therapeutic: group therapy in sociodrama and individual therapy in psychodrama. But if the educational implications are examined various useful pointers emerge.

1 An individual member of a sociodrama group will, (while he plays a specific role), insight into the progenitor of the role, emotionally as well as intellectually.
2 Through the acting out of the situation by the other members of the cast, he gains insight into the feelings and attitudes of others.
3 By placing him in the 'synthetic' situation of the sociodrama it enables him to look at the problem from a novel viewpoint.

Thus, developing from these antecedents we arrive at a definition[7] of role-playing as 'a spontaneous portrayal (acting out) of a situation, condition or circumstance by selected members of a learning group'.

Role-playing in adult education is concerned with relationships, attitudes, change of views. Its outstanding feature is the emotional impact experienced by the player or observer. Insights into the feelings, reactions and attitudes surrounding the situation in question are more likely to be gained than by merely reading about it or hearing a lecture.

WHEN SHOULD ROLE-PLAYING BE USED?

This question may best be answered by considering certain specific learning situations and the objectives they are aiming for.

1 A course is to be offered on 'Adolescence', designed particularly for the parents of children entering secondary schools. The presentation of the emotional tangle and ultra-sensitivity experienced by many adolescents might well take the form of role-playing. A selected group might, with the help of the teacher, 'work up' this piece of the course to be undertaken as their special responsibility. The personal hostility between child and parent so often a feature of the adolescent stage could be well illustrated, and subsequent discussion could offer reasons and solutions.
2 Local authority youth services have recently undergone a radical reorganisation, following the report of a specially constituted and widely based working party. Many youth leaders feel a sense of grievance. A training workshop session is organised in which individual youth leaders role-play the members of a working party constituted on the same lines as the original. The recommendations produced, and the dialogue and interchange during the proceedings, are carefully discussed after the role-playing is ended. Comparisons are drawn with the original report.
3 A meeting of newly appointed part-time teachers has been called

in order to offer them help and advice on the various classroom situations they are likely to encounter. Two or three contrasting student 'types' or groups are role-played by the advisers (organisers, principals, heads of department), and alternative approaches are discussed.

These three authentic and, as observed by the writer, successful cases illustrate certain distinct advantages of role-playing.

1 It encourages more active participation than many other discussion techniques; the novelty and challenge of the approach often stimulate people to comment who would otherwise just ride on the wave of dialogue produced by the more skilful talkers.
2 Problems of human behaviour and relationships can be presented in a way which can scarcely be rivalled by other, more traditional techniques.
3 The purely intellectual experience produced by most other discussion techniques is extended into an emotional experience.

There are considerable limitations, however, in the use of this technique in adult education.

1 Role-playing should not be employed when the educational objectives are complex; the insights aimed for should be in relation to clear-cut problems; paradoxically, it is seldom found satisfactory when there is only one answer.
2 There is some danger that the true educational objectives can become obscured by the involvement of the participants in the drama; the 'gimmick' aspect has to be guarded against. Alternatively, bad role-playing, unsuitable casting or confused production can destroy the whole learning situation.
3 It is advisable to avoid the use of role-playing if fear, anxiety or undue embarrassment is likely to be engendered in any member of the group.

A note of warning on the inappropriate use of role-playing was sounded by Brunner[8] in 1959.

> . . . . The technique of role-playing should not be uncritically accepted by adult educators. Research is needed to determine what sort of people, kinds of topic, purposes and situations lend themselves to its effective use, and to determine more precisely just what are the significant and effective factors in the role-playing.

While accepting Brunner's caveat as applying to any technique available to the educator, there is now a considerable body of experience associated with role-playing, and much of this has been carefully evaluated. The advantages and limitations previously noted in this chapter summarise the conclusions to date.

THE ROLE-PLAYING PROCESS

Role-playing as an educational technique involves a good deal more than the actual acting of a scene. The key person is the producer or leader, who is usually the teacher of the group but not necessarily so. He may undertake to define all the necessary details himself, or, better still, he may lead the group towards a consensus in dealing with each step in the procedure. At all stages he must bear in mind the characteristics of the group—their age, sex, background and known attitudes.

The major steps usually associated with role-playing are as follows:

1 defining the problem and establishing a situation;
2 determining the roles to be played;
3 casting the characters;
4 briefing the participants;
5 acting out the scene;
6 discussion and analysis.

Defining the Problem and Establishing a Situation
The problem to be elucidated should be clear-cut, significant and preferably close and important to the persons playing the roles or observing the performance. The situation in which the problem is projected should also be relatively simple, as complexities can distract attention from the main problem.

Determining the Roles to be Played
The involvement of the group in this step is often valuable and educationally productive. The dawning of insights into the problem can often be observed at this stage. The producer should take careful note of the characteristics of each role, and preferably he should write them down. The number of roles should not be too large, perhaps five major roles as a maximum.

Casting the Characters
The producer should not primarily seek acting ability, but rather empathy with the character involved. Nobody should be subjected to undue pressure to take a part, and it sometimes helps if the teacher himself takes a difficult or unpopular one.

Most of the roles, however, described in the particular problem at issue, fall into recognisable and important categories: information giver, information seeker, initiator, coordinator, goal-orientator, energiser, summariser, recorder, evaluator, encourager, follower, aggressor, recognition-seeker, distractor, play-boy, blocker. The teacher/producer will often recognise or arrange more than one of these categories in a role, but he may also have to assume several himself in order to ensure a full investigation of the basic problem.

Briefing the Participants

Briefing may be oral or written, but in the opinion of the writer the latter is preferable. Each player can be given a brief written synopsis of the role to be played, including the situation in which the dialogue and action will occur. It is useful to give a little time for quiet assimilation of this written material, followed by a short session of question and answer and discussion. This should not, however, determine the nature of the dialogue or action, otherwise the essential spontaneity of the technique is lost. Nothing comparable to the rehearsal of a formal production is required.

Acting out the Scene

The action should be a spontaneous development of the basic scenario presented in the briefing. It is important, however, to arrive at the right timing for the piece. From the writer's experience it frequently occurs that the teacher-producer will overestimate the length of time during which the roles and situation can be sustained. Even where all members of the group are actually playing roles (ie no audience) it is unwise to continue 'in role' for longer than one hour. Most situations will be able to be explored in substantially shorter periods of time. It may be necessary for the teacher to cut the piece rather earlier than expected, but an intervention will be required in any case once sufficient action has taken place for the group to analyse the situation.

In a few cases it may be useful to replay the scene, but this should be agreed beforehand. It may be possible to explore a different angle of the situation by varying slightly the roles or offering a change of stress in the original scenario. Replays, however, should be used very sparingly.

Discussion and Analysis

Following the cutting of the action, the tutor should firmly release the players from their roles and lead towards a discussion which analyses the action and quickly attempts to pin-point key features of the feelings of the players as well as examining important pieces of dialogue and action. It is important to try to seize these important emotive insights as soon as possible; all too frequently the members of the group will slip into other roles such as 'critic', 'analyst', 'deprecator' as they adopt the mental posture of a discussion group. Later the facts, principles, causes and effects can be discussed, and a thorough reinforcement of the learning situation can be undertaken

It is important in this final phase that the perception of the group (not least the teacher) should be turned towards the educational objectives of the exercise and towards the formulation of solutions or suggestions for action or follow-up. It is also easy to become so enamoured of the drama that the basic educational aims are completely lost.

SIMULATION TECHNIQUES

There is nothing very new about simulation techniques except the coining of the jargon umbrella-title by which they are now known. As Tansey and Unwin[9] have said, 'physicists have their ripple tanks, geographers have their wave-form tanks and little children have their dolls and toy soldiers. Simulation is within the experience of each one of us.'

What has happened since simulation began to be an in-word among educators is that attention has been focused on the potential of the techniques as an aid in education.

Indeed, several writers would place the role-playing technique as merely one of many variations on the simulation theme. The writer sees important differences, as well as similarities, in the two types of procedure.

It has been demonstrated that the bases of role-playing, especially as cultivated by Moreno, are therapy and spontaneity, whether in terms of individuals, groups or situations.

By contrast simulation methods always require a well-defined model[10] on which to proceed. They are usually strongly structured, that is to say that there are rules of procedure which limit the spontaneity of action and response.

Thomas[11] describes one of the earliest examples of simulation exercise in the *kriegspiel* or Prussian war game introduced in 1798. This simulation had rules, logically based on the normal conduct of battles, and used maps and later logistical tables. These war games were introduced into the British Army in 1872 and spread to the United States around the turn of the century.

But it was not until the 1950s that business and industrial education perceived the usefulness of simulation. The first business game was probably devised by the American Management Association in 1956. It was competitive, and was linked to an IBM650 computer which acted as scorekeeper. The participants took the roles of executives responsible for the decision-making of a number of competing firms producing a similar product. The effects of their decisions not only on their own interests but on those of their competitors were analysed and calculated within the framework of a number of mathematical models programmed into the computer. Thus continual assessment of the relative gains and losses of the competitors was available. Several later sophistications of this simulation have followed.

Games, or rule-bound procedures involving competition, are a common form of simulation, and it is frequently claimed that 'table' games such as 'Monopoly', 'Strategy' and other similar products are educational. The educator has to be quite certain of the overall aims and purposes of his work, and needs to be precise in identifying particular educational objectives for the employment of his time with his students. Indeed the whole aspect of strong competition usually associated with academic, business or war games has overtones which militate against realising the full educational benefit. Whenever a system is devised which produces one winner there are usually several losers. When the motivation and involvement of the participants is so strongly tied to the notion of winning this would seem to be a very unproductive procedure for the educator, especially in the long run. The more participative forms of simulation, or those where the student only competes against himself or the impersonal forces around him (for example in the Link Trainer for flying simulation), seem to offer more to the adult educator. While there is likely to be great appeal to youngsters in school in the notion of a competitive classroom game, it is less likely to excite adults. Also, as Tansey and Unwin found, there is a tendency to develop increasing concern about the skills of the competition rather than the incidental learning or educational goals.

It may be useful at this stage to give an example of two or three simulation exercises, all of which have been operated by the writer.

Decisions and Objectives

Students on a post-qualification, orientation-training course for youth leaders were given a copy of a leader's annual report which included financial accounts, notable incidents during the year, membership statistics and staffing and accommodation details for a typical urban youth club. The financial accounts showed a slight deficit.

They were then asked to make decisions in regard to five problems involving financial expenditure, heavy staff commitment, public relations and programme changes. Their decisions were recorded individually in the first place, and then again following discussion in groups of three. They were later asked to associate the decisions with certain organisational aims and objectives. Finally analysis of the procedure, including

G

overall scores on the decisions made and objectives chosen, was conducted by the teacher.

This exercise, based on the European Research Group on Management[12] 'Exercise Objectives', has been very well received by a wide variety of trainee youth service workers, and follow-up evaluations have shown its effectiveness in realising important educational goals.

Exercise Administrator

Geography students at a further education college were given a full description of situational, topographical, climatic and vegetational features of a fictional Pacific island. They were asked to arrive individually at various conclusions about agricultural possibilities, trade and navigation and industrial development. They were then formed into syndicate groups of three and asked to formulate policies for a mixed racial population aiming at optimum cultural and economic conditions. The final plans were compared, analysed and discussed under the guidance of a teacher.

In-tray Exercise

A group of part-time evening institute principals attending an inservice training conference was given a series of problems devised to simulate commonly occurring features of the work, and also to provide a basis for considering the objectives by which decisions can be guided. The problems were presented as if they arrived on the desk of the principal during one evening's work. Initially the group considered them individually; later it was split into small groups and a consensus of decision was required. The overall content and strength of decisions taken were subsequently analysed and discussed in plenary session.

PLANNING A SIMULATION EXERCISE

This is little different from the preliminaries involved in preparing other techniques, except that most of the work is required before the classroom situation is reached. The following steps are necessary.

1 Clear objectives must be defined in line with the overall aims of the course.
2 A realistic situation must be envisaged and described, in which the simulation can be presented.
3 Clear directions (rules) must be formulated for the procedures to be

followed. Time intervals are especially important and, if the simulation is presented in booklet form, specially clear directions are required as to when (and when not) to turn over pages.

4 The problems presented to the student should be in a form which requires consideration, involvement and commitment. The results should be recorded in the most succinct way possible.

5 The design should, if possible, incorporate some means of scoring or evaluation to assist the analysis. It should not involve any competitive element.

6 Timing of all stages is vital, for there will always be a tendency to overshoot the time-limits on sections and consequently to have to pinch on the last of the sequence. If this were to reduce the final analysis session it would militate strongly against reaching the designed educational goal.

Educational games and simulations have been published which can help the teacher to use this technique with his class.

In mathematics, Layman E. Allen[13] of the University of Chicago has been the most active designer of games. They are intended to teach specific concepts and are not intended to encourage creative ideas or to inculcate values. The most well known is the 'Wff'n Proof' game which has been promoted by a commercial educational publisher. Others of Allen's games include 'Equations', 'On Sets', the 'Real Numbers' game.

In international relations, games and simulations are often closer together than in other areas of study. 'Dangerous Parallel', devised by the Foreign Policy Association of New York[14] is not commercially available. The intention is that by demanding understanding of the complex inter-relationships and crises of the countries involved the students will develop a more analytical approach to international affairs. This game has been extended in its range of influence by being shown on an educational television network in the United States. Decisions of study groups playing the game can be telephoned into the studio, and the effects viewed immediately. Another similar game 'Crisis', is available commercially but involves fictional nation-states and an imaginary situation.

In vocational training, the 'Life Career' game, devised by Sarane Boocock[15] of Johns Hopkins University, is designed to present the decisions that people have to make at various crucial stages in their lives. This is one of the few games in which a statistically based evaluation has been attempted, and analyses so far indicate favourable results in decision training, information assimilation and factual learning. Its author sees its prime use ultimately as part of a package for vocational testing and counselling.

Civics has a number of simulations and games specifically designed to help in learning about society, the legislative process and the constitution. They include 'Democracy', 'Napoli' and 'Section'.[16]

Geography has been the subject most frequently involved in simulation and games designs in Britain; 'Dunstanbridge' and 'Micropolis'[16] are two such products.

Economics has attracted a number of designs, of which 'Consumer' and 'Economic System 915' are used for university teaching in the USA.

In Britain a notable contribution to communications teaching was worked out by John H. Smith[17] of Manchester University Extra-Mural Department. A full description of his 'North-Western Match Company' simulation exercise was published in *Adult Education* of September 1968. Again at Manchester, Ken Harrison and Barry Long[18] devised their 'Chip Game' which investigated group decisions and reactions in relation to the production side of industry. It allowed the teacher to introduce 'crises' into production procedures, requiring rapid reconsideration and new planning.

Enough experience has been gained to show that teachers can, to great advantage, introduce these simulation techniques into their schemes of work. They do not require large financial outlay, technical expertise or complex equipment. They are entirely within the professional control of the educator, nothing needs to be discarded (as in prepacked films, film strips or video tapes), and they have a high enjoyment factor associated with them.

Although this last (the 'fun' factor) may be regarded as suspect or even non-educational in some quarters, it is hoped that this will not deter teachers from trying these methods.

NOTES

1 Spencer, H. *The Principles of Psychology* (New York 1873)
2 Groos, K. (trans Baldwin, E. L.) *The Play of Man* (1901)
3 Ebbinghaus, H. (trans Meyer, M.) *Psychology, An Elementary Text* (Boston 1908)
4 Parsons, T., Bales, R. F. and Shils, E. *Working Papers in the Theory of Action* (Glencoe, Illinois 1953)
5 See Ruddock, R. 'Social factors in adult learning', *Adult Education,* 40 no 2 (1967)
6 Moreno, J. L. *Who shall survive?* (New York 1934); *Psychodrama 1* (New York 1946); *Psychodrama 2* (New York 1959). It is interesting to contrast Moreno's views with the highly structured role-playing stereotypes identified by the modern 'transactional analysis'. See Berne, Eric. *Games People Play* (1967)
7 See Bergevin, P., Morris, D. and Smith, R. M. *Adult Education Procedures* (New York 1963)

8 Brunner, E. de S. *An Overview of Adult Education Research* (Chicago 1959)
9 Tansey, P. J. and Unwin, D. *Simulation and Gaming in Education* (1969)
10 A model, in this context, is an abstraction, précis or scaled-down version of a real-life situation. It contains the essential inter-relation of the variables in the situation and should be designed so that an observer will not be confused by complexities in the original.
11 Thomas, C. J. *The Genesis and Practice of Operational Gaming* (Baltimore 1957)
12 European Research Group on Management (ERGOM). *A Program of Exercises for Management and Organisational Psychology*
13 Allen, L. E. 'Towards Autotelic Learning of Mathematical Logic', *Mathematics Teacher* (January 1963)
14 Foreign Policy Association. *Dangerous Parallel* (New York)
15 Boocock, Sarane. 'Simulation of a Learning Environment for Career Planning and Vocational Choice', *Proceedings of American Psychological Association* (September 1966)
16 Tansey, P. J. and Unwin, D. 'Academic Games Currently Being Marketed', *Bulletins on Gaming and Simulation* No 5 (Reading 1968)
17 Smith, John H. 'Teaching Communications—Active Methods', *Adult Education,* 41 no 5 (1968)
18 Harrison, K. and Long, B. E. L. 'The Chip Game', details available from the Department of Adult Education, The University, Manchester M13 9PL

9 Student Activity Outside the Classroom

Keith Jackson

The contributions which adult education may make to individual students' lives and to society at large have often been outlined. However, lack of research into teaching methods, and the scarcity of systematic descriptions of teachers' experience does not make it easy to translate broad aims into specific forms of organisation and teaching, as, for example, is proposed by the Nuffield projects in school mathematics. It is claimed that adult teachers are particularly concerned to relate their teaching to the lives and activities of their students, and this is certainly reflected in the subject matter of courses. Yet the literature on actual teaching methods reflects a rather conventional concern with the classroom, and places a strong emphasis on teaching rather than learning.

Until recently this literature has shown a bias towards those subjects associated with the 'responsible body' field of liberal adult education. In the rapidly expanding local education authority field in Britain, where the subject range is wider and where more attention is given to practical skills, accounts of developments and experiments and exhortations to colleagues have largely been the work of administrators and organisers, not teachers. This denies to anyone who attempts a survey of teaching practice the detailed examples which would sharpen comparisons between the teaching of liberal subjects and that of personal skills. However, sufficient evidence is beginning to appear to justify a claim that many of the principles which produce successful out-of-class activities apply to most subjects taught in adult education.[1]

Another point must be emphasised. The evening class conducted on one night a week for a series of weeks is not the only form of programme for an adult education course, although it is the most common. Greater flexibility of teaching method can often be achieved in other forms of programme or timetable. Consequently, organisers and teachers should constantly bear in mind the possibility of offering alternatives to the class programme or adding units to it. Single afternoon or whole-day

102

sessions, week-end schools, linked day or week-end conferences, residential weeks, day-release courses, extended evenings of more than one session are all possible. The intention in this chapter is to try to indicate which methods are best suited to a particular form of timetable arrangement.

There are a number of broad objectives which are common to all kinds of student activity outside the classroom.

These are:

The reinforcement of classroom learning.

Assessment and evaluation both by the student himself and the teacher.

Feedback to the teacher, so that his own teaching may improve. Learning of new information and skills.

Increased attention to the needs of separate individuals and groups within the class.

The most common forms of activity are:

Individual work.

Small groups and project work.

Class projects, exhibitions, surveys and histories.

Class visits.

There are also approaches to adult education, including self-supporting classes and work with autonomous groups, which are more independent of classroom teaching, and these will be reviewed briefly.

INDIVIDUAL WORK

Reading

Experienced teachers continue to be amazed at the wide variations in age, educational background, experience, current situations and aspirations, as well as personal characteristics, which are found in adult classes. One very important way of dealing with this variety is to allocate work to each student to be completed outside the classroom. A great deal can be achieved by creating an atmosphere in which students are constantly made aware that a course will be of much greater value if their commitment is greater than the mere hours in which a class meets.

In the final analysis reading is for most subjects by far the most important kind of individual work. It is essential that an arrangement be made for appropriate books to be made easily available. In most kinds of responsible body classes a book box is provided, with a range of texts which the teacher has selected as being essential or particularly appropriate for the course. When classes are held in an adult centre it is often better to set aside shelves in the college library for each class within the centre. 'Book boxes are emergency rations. In 1967 adult students have a right to expect and to handle a more balanced, well stocked larder'.[2] Bookstalls can also be arranged for students to buy texts, particularly paperback editions.

All forms of work outside the classroom gain from a careful introduction and explanation by the teacher. This is true of reading. Book boxes should not be left in a corner of the room as a sort of 'lucky dip' tub which students may hastily sample at the beginning or the end of classes. Time should be set aside to describe the different kinds of book available. Brief resumés of contents and points of view can be given. The different uses of different kinds of book such as reference works, detailed monographs or narrative accounts, should be explained. Important chapters and sections of books can be indicated. Adult students with full-time jobs often have a limited time available for reading. In many subjects it will be better that something is read than nothing at all.

As stressed in Chapter 6, the adult teacher should ask himself how well students can deal with books. Do they use the contents lists and indexes intelligently? Are they able to grasp the general argument of a book or chapter by reading through it quickly? Do they realise that different styles, treatment and subject matter demand differences in reading approach? For example, students may be discouraged in philosophy and technical subjects if they do not realise that tight arguments and explanations demand more time and attention than narrative exposition.

Writing and Creative Work

'Just as the habit of regular reading is one that should be carefully fostered, so is the habit of regular writing'.[3] Like reading, it should be an expected accompaniment to a course. Problems often arise because written work is regarded in too formal and unimaginative a manner. It is better to view written work as only one of many kinds of individual student activity designed to give an opportunity for learning and creativity not possible in the classroom, and the following points should be read with that in mind.

There are a number of principles to follow when asking students to produce individual work. It should be carefully related to their present abilities, resources and time available; it should be varied not stereotyped, taking into account students' interests, particular skills, current situations or opportunities; at the same time it should be clearly defined so that the students know what is expected of them; completed work should be taken seriously and not given cursory recognition; finally, it is likely to make the maximum contribution to an individual's progress, as well as to that of the whole class, if it is carefully integrated into the course and, whenever possible, the classroom teaching situation.

The point about ability and resources is an obvious one; it is often unrealistic, for example, to ask for a formal essay from many students. Initially it may be best to ask them for a few notes, composed fairly casually but beginning the process of getting pen to paper. These can be on the subject matter of a book, on a visit to an exhibition, on a film, television programme or a substantial newspaper article. It is often appropriate to suggest that students keep a notebook to record class work. As with reading, guidance in note-taking will usually be helpful.

Short answers to uncomplicated questions and even questionnaires should not be despised. The latter can be used to test factual knowledge, but are even more valuable for testing understanding of key points. They can also help a teacher to get to know the class.

Once sufficient momentum has been achieved in the class as a whole and individuals are gaining confidence, they can be asked specifically to prepare a few notes in order to introduce a topic during the class. Richard Hoggart shows the attitude of a successful adult teacher when he describes the way in which he allocated such work to students.

> In the first three or four weeks I let volunteers take on the prepared notes. But I find it is important to switch from this approach before I have run right through the volunteers and am left with half a dozen students looking at each other in a frightened way. By the end of these three or four weeks I am beginning to know them pretty well and can begin to suggest that the coming week's topic might well suit Mr B. and that I'll be glad if he'll take it on, and will talk to him about it after the class if he wishes.[4]

In classes on the creative arts, including literature, no opportunity should be lost to encourage students to compose a piece of systematic analysis or criticism. Photographs and slides may be contributed by students in appropriate classes, although teachers must beware of extended holiday reminiscences. For many kinds of social studies a diary can be kept to illustrate forms of social interaction.

For some students and some classes the formal essay has precisely the same advantages as in other fields of education. Rigid and unimaginative questions will get rigid and unimaginative answers. The strength which adult education has gained through its traditional separation from the formalised system of examinations and qualifications are valuable here. Subject material may be as idiosyncratic and personally chosen as any student wishes. The voluntary nature of adult classes makes a fair degree of motivation and interest likely, even taking into account the many social and non-educational factors which lead students to join. Hence if, eventually, essay writing becomes acceptable to students, it is worth exploiting the opportunity to develop powers of argument and linguistic skills.

Some indication of achievement will make many courses more satisfying for both teachers and students. Written work and particularly some form of essay should not be underestimated as a means of discovering how far students have grasped a subject and when factual knowledge or understanding of arguments is weak. Many students themselves value individual written work because it gives them a sense of progress and achievement. Comments such a 'I am amazed how much I know once I begin to write' and 'I didn't realise what you were getting at until I tried to put it on paper' are much more common than those bemoaning difficulties.

It is best to assume that producing a piece of work is regarded by the student as a considerable achievement. Of course fluency will vary, but many adults will produce many successive drafts before work is submitted, even if it is not very long or complex in form. The absence of comment will, at the least, be discourteous and it may lead to discouragement, lack of confidence or decline in interest. For the same reason any opportunity for a word of praise, even to less able students, should not be missed. Students will also be encouraged when their work is brought into the discussions of the class as a whole in a constructive manner.

GROUP WORK[1]

Projects, Surveys, Histories and Exhibitions

The second basic form of work outside the classroom is the group project of one kind or another. Most attention is usually devoted to projects which involve all the members of the class. However, it is also worth while to consider briefly the merits of other forms of group work.

It is now common practice in schools to break a class into small groups which work independently. There are advantages in applying the same method to adult teaching. For example, individuals may be encouraged by working alongside friends, and a valuable debate and exchange of views can result from each group discussing the findings with the rest of the class.

Small groups can be given short-term or long-term tasks. An example of the former is when the teacher sets a number of open questions which groups are to discuss in order to pool experience and clarify their minds before returning to the full class for a final debate. The system works best during half-day or all-day sessions, or as part of a short residential course when the timetable can be suitably arranged. There may be a short introductory session for the whole class, during which the context can be set and the questions carefully explained, a period when the groups disperse to tackle the questions, and a reporting back session to round off the exercise. This approach works very well when there are moral or philosophical issues to be discussed or policy questions of current concern. Conference and 'workshops' for local voluntary association leaders or social workers (or adult educators) are most appropriate settings. Courses dealing with such subjects are intended to clarify ideas as much as to present information, and it is particularly important that every student should feel able to express himself.

The same general principle may be applied to weekly courses. Topics can be allocated to small groups for fact finding and discussion before they contribute a joint paper or report to the whole class. Since students are often more conservative than teachers, they may expect the all-too-common lectures followed by desultory questions and discussion, and this approach can be used to loosen the structure of the class meeting itself. A meeting can be devoted to groups working at their separate tasks with the teacher giving advice only if asked, and encouragement where needed. Later class meetings often benefit from the greater informality introduced in this way.

Adult students are only likely to respond to this kind of approach if it is prepared carefully and taken seriously. Topics should be chosen which are genuinely appropriate to the treatment. Individual reading will be stimulated by this kind of group project. When groups present their material it should genuinely contribute to the original programme and not be an obvious 'optional extra' added as a sort of gimmick.

CLASS PROJECTS

Surveys, Construction Projects

When a whole class is concerned with a single project of some length, the style and method of teaching is usually changed substantially at some stage. The teacher's role becomes close to that of a consultant. Sometimes a class and project can run separately and interdependently, so that the teacher performs two roles. In the following example of a social survey, from which general principles behind good project work clearly emerge, the class decided to carry out a social survey, to study sociology by 'doing' rather than by 'being told'.

> That some 7,500,000 people in this country should be living at or below the national assistance scales (since shown, by the Ministry of

Social Security's own survey, to be a considerable underestimate)
was not only shocking but incredible to many members of Nottingham University's 1965-66 course on British social structure, 'The
anatomy of Britain.' Out of this class, therefore, arose the idea
that it would be useful to investigate conditions in Nottingham to
discover whether the local picture was compatible with the findings
of Brian Abel-Smith and Peter Townsend.[6]

This is an excellent example of the ideal situation where a project
arose directly out of the study needs of a class. Sometimes more prompting by a teacher may be needed, often new recruits may be added to
the class, attracted by the exercise, as they were in this survey of St
Anne's, Nottingham.

During this exercise students were from the first involved in a full
discussion of the project. Their own dissatisfaction with preconceived
notions of poverty led them to see the need for a survey which was not
too narrowly based. As they were involved in the preparation and
learned the nature and limitations of questionnaires, schedules and other
means of collecting information, they could see the value of keeping
the project manageable, of not trying to answer all the questions that
occurred to them. Later, they understood more precisely the nature of
statistics and the varying reliability of witnesses. This opportunity to
understand the methodology of a subject rather than merely knowing
about its end-products is invaluable. Its importance is common to all
subjects that are taught in adult education. Full involvement in the
early preparation also helps to prevent later stages becoming too narrowly
mechanical for those involved, thus maintaining their commitment and
increasing their capacity to learn from what they are doing.

As the project got under way, students were given every opportunity
to use their own professional positions and other social situations.
Public officials were able to set up 'separate but parallel investigations
into the records of their own departments, thus producing a number of
related profiles of the area'. An even more imaginative and somewhat
courageous contribution was that of the housewife who fed her family
for a week on the diet suggested by Rowntree and Lavers in their
Poverty and the Welfare State (1951).[7] During the week 'they ingested
a fair quantity of sago and lentils and six pounds of swedes (they were
all much relieved when the experiment was successfully concluded)'.[8]

Throughout the survey the class read widely, not only books but also
detailed reports of other relevant projects. They were not restricted to a
narrow task. The opportunity was taken to extend knowledge and understanding, not just to complete the project. It was also intended that the
results themselves should be fed back into the class. Discussions were
planned with appropriate officials and elected representatives. Just as

important was the expectation that discussions would continue within the class on the basic concepts involved in the idea of poverty and its implications for social action. Intensive debate was anticipated, for now the group would be 'armed with the data collected in the survey'.

Considerable space has been devoted to this project because further information about it is easily available to the reader and because it illustrates most of the principles which can be applied to any class project. It arose out of the class; students were fully involved at every stage; and it was used to broaden the educational opportunities of class members, not to reduce them to technical assistants of a teacher eager to pursue an investigation.

LOCAL STUDIES

W. G. Hoskins in his *Fieldwork in Local History* emphasises how appropriate this subject is to adult education and how adult classes have made a genuine contribution to its development. 'It is hardly too much to say that adult education classes are one of the most vigorous growing points for the serious study of local history in this country'.[9]

In recent years an impressive monument to this contribution is *A History of Nidderdale* produced by a Leeds University Extra-Mural Department and Workers' Educational Association tutorial class. In a paper presented to the 1968 Conference of the Universities Council for Adult Education, Bernard Jennings, the class teacher emphasised how the project developed directly out of the interest of the class and how it was never allowed to become narrow and mechanical. He particularly warned against the danger that some members of a class might be allocated only menial tasks, and therefore make very little progress over the period of the project. A teacher's responsibility to each of his students is not lessened by the different role he occupies in the context of a project; group pressures to complete the work can make his concern for the individual even more important. Teachers themselves must also avoid the temptation to consider classes as task forces to help them follow their own academic interests, imposing their own urgency and timetables on the group.

Local studies of many kinds provide excellent opportunities for class projects. A list of the basic subject areas involved would include social studies, physical and social geography, economics, history, politics, archaeology, literature, geology, photography, painting and natural history.

Another popular subject which also has connections with a locality but which has many other virtues in adult education is archaeology. Out of this have developed specialised sub-divisions such as industrial archaeology.[10] It combines a discussion of social, economic, political and other historical topics with a scientifically orientated methodology, and it presents convenient opportunities for practical involvement. No teacher of archaeology will need much prompting to develop a whole range of out-of-classroom activities. Frequently, as in summer digs, the classroom can be jettisoned altogether. However, all the points which have been made for other subjects apply equally to archaeology. Indeed the danger of a group of adult students, or part of a group, being demoted to labourers for keen archaeologists is even greater. Teaching must not be lost in the process of achieving the more concrete objectives of a dig.

VISITS AND EXHIBITIONS

It is sometimes said that the historian's best tools are a strong stick and a stout pair of boots. Actually seeing, like actually doing, is a powerful source of learning for any student.

It is not difficult for most teachers to arrange visits which would make abstract material more concrete and introduce stimulating new experiences. Art and architecture, archaeology, town-planning and natural history spring most quickly to mind, but both industrial relations and chemistry can benefit equally from a visit to industrial establishments. Council debates are open to members of politics classes as they are to other members of the public. A discussion of industrial relations in the mining industry gains substantially if students have actually been down a pit. Likewise slides are no substitute for real paintings in art appreciation classes.

Visits are always most successful in educational terms if they are carefully planned and used to the full in the course as a whole. It is not impossible in some subjects to build a whole programme of instruction around a visit so that the concrete and actual takes the centre of the stage. This has been particularly valuable in some courses and residential schools on drama or literature. J. R. Williams put forward what he called an ideal sequence, which admirably illustrates a basic approach; it is offered here as a guide rather than a detailed prescription.

1 A play is chosen which is to be performed locally.
2 Everybody reads it.
3 It is subjected to class analysis.
4 The group attends a theatrical performance.
5 There is a post mortem on the performance and a final discussion.[11]

The same approach might be used for art classes centred around major exhibitions of painting or sculpture, or the planning and architecture of a new town or redevelopment areas. Even when the visit is less central to the course as a whole, it is valuable to give it as much treatment of this kind as is possible.

In recent years visits abroad have grown increasingly popular; language courses obviously benefit, as do courses in history or art—the Renaissance can still come alive in Florence or Venice. But a wide range of social studies should not be neglected; adult students are able to gain a great deal from observation and comparison. Some WEA districts, extra-mural departments and local education authority adult centres have arranged composite foreign summer schools, involving a number of subjects including history, sociology, art, architecture and literature, and incorporating substantial preparation in the form of a class or a series of day conferences in the weeks preceding the summer school.[12] Under such circumstances students are willing to do a great deal of work and not just take a holiday abroad. Many different kinds of visits are possible. The Confédération de la Famille Rurale organises study visits in Western Europe for many young French adults, mainly from peasant homes, and it is claimed that these undertakings have had observable effects in stimulating needed changes in the French rural economy.[13] In Britain, WEA districts have arranged exchange visits with parties of trade unionists in Western European countries, although it would take courage to claim any effects on British industry.

Any kind of visit adds considerably to an adult teacher's work. There is a greater degree of preparation in order to ensure the relevance of a visit to a particular course; written material may well be required for adequate guidance of the visitors; there is the conduct of the visit and subsequent evaluation of the information and experiences students have gained. Even more than class projects, this underlines the need for more full-time workers in adult education, both as teachers and administrators.

ADULT EDUCATION WITHOUT A CLASSROOM

The dominance of the classroom in adult education traditions can obscure the fact that learning by adults also takes place in much less structured situations and will always do so. This is not the place to review such informal educational activities in detail, but a reference is appropriate. It sets out-of-class activities in the right context and points the way to even greater flexibility on the part of teachers, organisers and administrators.

In Britain many voluntary organisations have a strong educational concern. Trade unions and the various women's organisations achieve a great deal without forming a class or a formal instruction group. The National Federation of Community Associations places great stress on creating an informal, open-ended learning situation in community centres,[14] while the Cambridgeshire Village Colleges and other community adult education centres are pioneering a slightly more purposefully educational version of the good community centre's lively and self-governing voluntary groups.

Although the Adult School Union has been responsible for the formation of many autonomous study groups, one must go outside Britain for examples of the systematic development of this form of adult education, midway between the formal class and the voluntary recreational association. The Swedish study circles frequently achieve a considerable degree of internal autonomy: 'the participants decide when they will meet, what they will study and how it will be done; . . . All leaders must refrain from the usual teacher-pupil relationship'.[15]

Systems of this kind are most common in countries where long distances between centres, or economic factors, make formal adult education difficult to provide. They are significant, however, for other situations because they indicate a role for the adult educator different from that of a classroom teacher. This role is expanded further when adult education is associated with a range of activities usually described as community development.

An important element in community development is the encouraging of groups of people to come together to define their community's problems or needs, from bus shelters to youth clubs and recreational groups, and to work out means by which these needs may be met. In Britain this process is commonly seen as a form of social work, partly because of the concentration of activity in areas with widely recognised social problems. However, the techniques and resources of adult education have a valuable part to play, and those who deploy them can be encouraged by the possibility that community development work may enable them to contact a wider variety of people than the normal methods of adult education.[16] For this reason, and because problems of leisure are beginning to be formulated in many neighbourhoods which are more clearly within the traditional province of adult education than some problems tackled by community development, it is probable that the two fields of activity will find new common ground in Britain, as has been the case in other countries.

In parts of North America, especially in rural areas, adult education is often cast entirely in the mould of community development.[17] University extension has included many different approaches. One writer, for example, describes functional extension as follows:

Encompassing what are called 'educational services', 'community development' and 'applied research', this type of university extension represents the adaptation of university resources to the needs and interest of off-campus youth and adults without regard to age, sex, religion or previous academic experience; such consultations may be rendered to individuals, groups, organisations and agencies.[18]

In Britain Goetschius[19] has recently described community development work in London housing estates, where groups were encouraged to tackle local problems in their own fashion. Although he is primarily concerned with community development as a form of social work, he identifies tasks which can also be performed in the context of adult education. While the groups he describes are entirely autonomous, they need to learn skills, to receive information and direction to sources of information, and to be given help and support. The role of the teacher is replaced by a combination of roles assumed by single individuals or by more than one in a team. There is that of consultant, or what is sometimes called 'resource-person',[20] and of co-ordinator, and also the role of non-directive group worker[21] helping people systematically to think through the nature of problems and needs and to consider alternative solutions. In this field, as in project work, but in a much more flexible and informal manner, adults learn through doing rather than being told. Many who might never attend formal classes can be approached on their own ground, dealing with matters of direct concern to them.

Imaginative experiment is vital in any form of adult education which aims to engage students in ways other than waiting for them to come to classes. In a recent edition of *Adult Education,* Long[22] describes an experiment that extends informality beyond working with fairly structured, autonomous groups. Noticing how crowds gathered around engineering and building contractors' operations, and how platforms and observation posts were often provided, Long aimed to provide continuous adult education facilities at an archaeological excavation. He set up an information and instruction centre at the site, hoping to add a new dimension to the common curiosity and interest he had observed. The teacher equipped himself, through a rapid course of background reading and through the help of the excavation leader, to answer the different kinds of question that he anticipated would arise. Long comments in conclusion that 'one feels that adult educators are a little reluctant to step outside the classroom and make learning opportunities of unstructured situations.'

H

CONCLUSION

The most important principles that can be drawn from a review of different kinds of student activity outside the classroom but within relatively formal courses are:

Out-of-class activities should grow naturally out of activities *in* the classroom.

The activity must be carefully thought out and prepared.

The students should be carefully introduced to and, if necessary, prepared for the form of activity.

The teacher must recognise when his role changes during the exercise and act accordingly, helping whenever required.

The activity should be integrated with the rest of the course.

The teacher must ensure that the exercise is completed satisfactorily, with appropriate comment and any advice about further work which may be required. Students' work, whether as individuals or as groups, should not be allowed to fade away indecisively.

The same principles can be applied to the more informal means of teaching where the outside activity dominates or replaces the formal course. Careful preparation, readiness to help when required, and attention to whatever follow-up is appropriate are still necessary for success. In addition it is particularly important in this field that the teacher attempts to clarify his educational objectives. What is he hoping students will learn, and at what point? He can then more easily determine what resources are required and how readily available they should and could be.

However, it is a commonplace in educational sociology to point out that there are many factors in an educational system which make it difficult for newly graduated, trained teachers to apply conscientiously the methods they have recently been taught. So it is appropriate to indicate in this conclusion some of the difficulties which are likely to be encountered by those teachers and organisers who aim to extend the range and effectiveness of adult education ouside the classroom. Both traditional attitudes and some present forms of organisation present obstacles. The wise practitioner will be aware of these and be prepared to deal with the problems.

The classroom situation is by far the most familiar model for an education activity. The responsible body tradition of adult education has for a long time further emphasised the role of the teacher. In local authority adult education, 'the basis of the evening institute is class teaching'.[23] The results of these traditions can be that teachers are faced with blank incomprehension when asking for additional facilities for other kinds of work. Indeed, the resources are often not available because they have not previously been requested.

Organisational and administrative arrangements have tended to ossify the traditions. This is particularly true of the physical arrangements for adult education and its substantial reliance on part-time teachers. There are by no means enough purpose-built centres or even centres which can be easily adapted for adult purposes. Libraries, properly equipped activity rooms and so on are the exception. Administrative facilities are often negligible. The contributions of the London City Institutes and other adult education centres, both residential and non-residential to experimentation in teaching methods have been substantial and indicate the difficulties which must be tackled under other circumstances when such facilities are not available.

More is required to effect a system of education than the skill, energy and willingness of individual teachers. Administrators and policy-makers must contribute. More full-time teachers and organisers are certainly required.[24]

Until more is known about the way in which adults learn, the precise contribution of activities outside the classroom cannot be dogmatically asserted. It is true, however, that those teachers who encourage such student work are rarely disappointed by its value and that those who have experimented with new forms of activity have been encouraged by the possibilities which emerge. Adult education should not ignore recent developments in primary and secondary education where the accent is on discovery. 'The need for carefully ordered, stimulating presentation is in no way minimised but the insistent requirement is that it must not take the form of a closed system'.[25]

NOTES

1 See *Visual Education* published monthly by the National Committee for Audio-Visual Aids in Education ; and *Vocational Aspect of Further Education* published three times a year by the Colleges of Education (Technical)
2 Clough, I. E. A., Rice, D. J. and Luckham, B. 'Book Boxes: Pro and Con', *Adult Education,* 40 no 3 (1967)
3 Raybould, S. G. *The Approach to WEA Teaching* (1947), 25
4 Hoggart, R. 'Some Notes on Extra-Mural Teaching', *Adult Education,* 33 no 4 (1960)
5 See also Ch 6
6 Coates, K. S. and Silbern, R. L. 'Urban Renewal—a social survey', *Adult Education,* 40 no 5 (1967), 1150. See also *Basingstoke: A Social Survey* (WEA Southern District 1966), and Broady, M. 'The Maidstone Project', *Social Service Quarterly,* (Spring 1966)

7   Rowntree, S. and Lavers, P. *Poverty and the Welfare State* (1951)
8   Coates and Sibern. 'Urban Renewal . . .'
9   Hoskins, W. G. *Fieldwork in Local History* (1967) quoted in a review by the same author of Munby, L. M. (ed). *East Anglian Studies* (Cambridge) in *Adult Education,* 41 no 5 (1969)
10 Webster, G. 'Archaeology in Adult Education', *Adult Education,* 32 no 4 (1960), 166-78 ; Corcoran, J. X. W. P. 'Archaeology' in Dees, N. (ed). *Approaches to Teaching Adults* (Oxford 1965) ; Parsons, D. 'Discovery Learning in Archaeology', *Adult Education,* 41 no 4 (1968)
11 Williams, J. R. 'Interpreting Drama', *Adult Education,* 33 no 5 (1961), 256
12 Maylor, W. D. 'Study Visits abroad by Air', *Adult Education,* 33 no 4 (1961) ; Jones, H. A. and Hay, M. 'The Liberal Approach in a Large Centre', in *On Teaching Foreign Languages to Adults,* a symposium edited by Lowe, M. and J. (Oxford 1965) ; Styler, W. E. *An Anglo-American Experiment* (Hull 1969)
13 Hutchinson, E. M. 'Adult Education', in *Techniques of Teaching* vol 3 : *Tertiary Education,* Peterson, A. D. C. (ed). (Oxford 1965), 129
14 National Federation of Community Associations, *Creative Living* (1967)
15 Hutchinson, E. M. 'Adult Education . . .' 119-20, quoting Bergevin, P. *Adult Education in Sweden* (Indiana)
16 Riches, G. 'Working Through Housing Estates', *Adult Education,* 39 no 6 (1967)
17 *Adult Leadership,* a journal published monthly, except July and August, by the Adult Education Association of the USA, devotes considerable space to community development and associated activities
18 Shannon, T. J. and Schoenfeld, C. A. *University Extension* (New York 1965) 4-5
19 Goetschius, G. W. *Working with Community Groups* (1968)
20 Hutchinson, E. M. 'Adult Education . . .', 121, describing the 'servicing tutor', in New South Wales.
21 James, W. 'Group Dynamic Theories', *Adult Education,* 37 no 3 (1964) and no 4 (1964)
22 Long, B. E. L. 'Education on Site', *Adult Education,* 41 no 4 (1968)
23 Edwards, H. J. *The Evening Institute* (1961), 168
24 This point is spelt out for a particular situation in an adult education centre by Gilbert, H. in 'A view about the Arts', *Adult Education,* 40 no 3 (1967) ; see also Hutchinson. 'Adult Education . . .', 128
25 Richmond, W. K. *The Teaching Revolution* (1967), 60

FURTHER READING

Cole, G. D. H. *The Tutor's Manual* (1919)
Morgan, B., Holmes, G. E. and Bundy, C. E. *Methods in Adult Education* (Danville, Illinois 1960)
Solomon, D., Bezdeck, W. E. and Rosenberg, L. *Teaching Styles and Learning* (Chicago 1963)
Peterson, A. D. C. (ed). *Techniques of Teaching,* vol 3 : *Tertiary Education* (Oxford 1965)

Lowe, M. and J. *On Teaching Foreign Languages to Adults* (Oxford 1965)

Broady, M. 'Teaching as Investigation', in Rogers, J. (ed). *Teaching on Equal Terms* (1969)

Dees, N. (ed). *Approaches to Adult Teaching* (Oxford 1965)

Baker, W. P. 'Informal Adult Education', in Raybould, S. C. (ed). *Trends in English Adult Education* (1959)

Marriott, S. 'Student-Centred Teaching', *Adult Education,* 40 no 4 (1967)

Kuenstler, P. H. K. *Social Group Work in Great Britain* (1958)

Goetschius, G. W. *Working with Community Groups* (1969)

Biddle, W. W. and L. J. *The Community Development Process* (New York 1965)

Shannon, T. J. and Schoenfeld, C. A. *University Extension* (New York 1965)

Batten, T. R. and Batten, Madge. *The Non-Directive Approach in Group and Community Work* (Oxford 1967)

Batten, T. R. *Communities and their Development* (Oxford 1957)

Munby, L. M. (ed). *East Anglian Studies* (Cambridge 1968)

10 Teaching Aids

Michael D. Stephens and Gordon W. Roderick

One of the significant features of the present world, as Marshall McLuhan points out, is the decline in the influence of the written word and the growing power of aural and other visual stimuli, with the result that students today may find themselves in a much more stimulating environment outside the classroom than inside.

The effectiveness of a teacher depends on the degree and diversity of skill he has in communicating his material to his students; until recently this was based almost entirely on classroom lectures supplemented by suitable reading material and blackboard instruction. However, over the last decade or so an increasing range of instructional media have become available to the teacher and a revolution is going on in educational circles as new techniques are being experimented with at different educational levels. In some quarters there has been a tendency to regard new techniques with certain misgivings, for the introduction of some of them has been accompanied by exaggerated claims and the impression is sometimes created that the teacher may become superfluous. In their eagerness to convert others, enthusiasts may in some instances have overstated their case, and there may be a feeling among some teachers that anyone who does not use audio-visual aids is no longer an effective teacher and, conversely, that anyone who teaches with the liberal assistance of aids is, ipso facto, a good teacher. The criterion, however, must always be effective communication, and this holds true regardless of whether audio-visual aids are being used or not.

The introduction of any new tool or technique must be judged in relation to the particular topic being taught. The teacher must ask ' Do I need any kind of aid? Will an aid help me to achieve any objective or make the teaching of this topic more effective?' If this is found to be the case the next question is 'What particular aid do I need?' For many teachers this may mean little or no change in the traditional pattern of teaching, whereas for others a whole range of techniques may help in the communication of their subject material in a more effective manner by supplementing textbook and blackboard.

Most teachers now accept that audio-visual aids are neither unneces-sary frills nor substitutes for the teacher, but are useful and in some cases essential adjuncts. They can

enrich and enliven teaching;

stimulate the student's desire to learn;

assist the learning process by making the assimilation and memorising of material easier;

help to hold attention;

induce greater acquisition and longer retention of information;

illustrate and clarify non-verbal images and symbols and quantitative relationships;

show processes, events and objects which may be inaccessible to many students;

bring a wide variety of experts into the classroom;

produce standardised material of unvarying quality;

free the teacher from routine repetitional tasks so that he can devote more time and energy to more profitable ones;

make learning available to wider audiences.

Audio-visual aids make good teachers better but are poor compensa-tions for inadequately thought-out teaching programmes. To be used to their best advantage they must be applied with care and thought. It is essential to combine their use one with another and to integrate them with traditional methods of instruction and not develop a slavish adher-ence to one particular technique. Skilful juxtaposition and combination of all the media and techniques available is called for. A sophisticated degree of selection is required and the basic philosophy should be, as one American writer so aptly put it, 'The right aid at the right time in the right place in the right manner.'

Further, if audio-visual aids are to be used there must be a thorough preparation beforehand. For instance, if a film is to be shown it is not good enough to say 'We are now going to see a film'; the teacher must be completely familiar with the film and must prepare the students so that they know what to look for and are conversant with the vocabulary or jargon in the spoken commentary etc. Likewise there must be ade-quate follow-up study of any audio-visual material, for the acquisition of facts or information is merely the first step in most learning situations.

At their best, audio-visual aids are a great help in the learning process, but too much reliance on them is harmful. The teacher must always be gauging the degree of inattention and boredom of the students and be prepared to modify his method, and he must judge the propitious moment for introducing a new technique. The impetus of learning must be maintained and switching from one technique to another, for example from slides to blackboard, and as a result having to put on the lights, forces the class to reorientate and helps to keep them alert.

Many teachers of adult classes are at a serious disadvantage, for they are not employed during the daytime in the institutions in which they teach at night. They cannot ensure the ready availability of equipment at the premises or the suitability of their own equipment to the accommodation provided. University extra-mural lecturers, WEA and other teachers of adults who use borrowed premises soon learn to turn their cars into mobile audio-visual aids centres transporting around the countryside blackboard, projectors and screen, a selection of electrical plugs and extension leads, screwdrivers etc. Even so, it is no easy matter in Britain to obtain overhead projectors and cine projectors outside the major towns. Part-time teachers employed by the local authorities complain that their demands for equipment meet with little success, but they may in the future obtain help from the audio-visual aids officers appointed by some authorities, whose function is to offer advice and help. Unfortunately, of 146 local education authorities 30 only have so far appointed audio-visual advisers.

Despite the many handicaps and obstacles encountered by anyone in adult education who seeks to enrich and to increase the efficiency of his teaching, the final result is rewarding and it is worth remembering that in many cases adult students, many of whom have been out of contact with formalised learning for many years, need more help than conventional students.

The range of audio-visual aids now available is indicated in the table. It is not the function of this chapter to give detailed and comprehensive descriptions of every piece of equipment, but rather to give a broad overall picture and to highlight one or two of the more exciting developments of recent times.

TABLE 1

AUDIO-VISUAL AIDS

VISUAL	AUDIO	AUDIO-VISUAL
Pictorial aids	Tape recorder	Slide and film strip
Blackboard	Record player	projector
Flannelgraphs		Film projector
Plastigraphs		Closed circuit
Magnetic boards		television
Episcope		Electronic video
Diascope		recording
Epidiascope		
Overhead projector		

NON-PROJECTED AIDS

Pictorial aids

Among pictorial aids, graphics and wall charts have important parts to play. The term graphics represents a group of instructional materials which present facts and ideas clearly through a combination of drawings, words and pictures and comprise graphs, charts, diagrams, posters, cartoons and comic figures.

Graphs represent numerical or statistical data in a visual form. The most commonly used is the line graph, but other forms are bargraphs, where the data is represented by vertical or horizontal bars, circle or pie graphs, which are divided into shaded sectors each representing a component part of some whole. Picture graphs (isotypes) have picture-like figures instead of bars or lines. The principal function of graphs is to present comparative information quickly and simply, so when a graph is intricate and difficult to interpret the object of showing it is defeated. Very detailed and extensive data are best explained in the form of a number of simple graphs rather than as a single complex graph. This principle of simplicity should always be observed, and approximations are better than precise amounts. Graphs are summarising devices and are best used in the middle or at the end of a lesson when the basic information has been conveyed to the students.

Charts, to be effective, must be simple, clear, in attractive colours and the lettering must be large enough. A large range of commercially-produced charts are available and they fall into different categories, but the ones must commonly used are the tree and stream charts. Tree charts show development from a base composed of several roots which lead into a single trunk. The branches represent developments and relationships. Such a chart may represent the genealogy of a family. A stream chart may show, for example, a variety of elements combining to form one product. In making home-made charts too much information or detail should not be conveyed, as it leads to confusion. It must be visible from a distance and lines should have a minimum thickness of $\frac{1}{8}$in at 25ft and $\frac{3}{16}$in at 50ft and lettering a minimum size of 1in high at 25ft and 2in high at 50ft.

Pictures and charts help to vitalise learning and can make abstractions meaningful. But to be effective they must be well prepared, wisely selected and used sparingly. They must be simple and have good colour contrasts. Studies show that blue, green and red are the most preferred colours; orange, red and blue have the greatest attention value; and yellow, green and orange have the greatest luminosity or brightness. It is preferable when selecting colours to use natural colour for realism, bright colours and strong contrasts for effect and warm bright colours for mood and atmosphere. These remarks on colours also apply to flannelgraphs and plastigraphs, which are discussed later.

Mobiles are wall charts with a difference. Instead of pictures lying static on a flat wall surface, these hang separately and independently on fine threads where they can move.

Often the best aid is a three-dimensional model which can provide interior views of objects such as machinery, car engines, sections of the ear, tooth or heart. They can reduce large objects or enlarge small ones such as an insect to suitable viewing size. They have the added advantage that they can be dismantled and reassembled.

The Blackboard

It is a matter for continuous surprise that blackboards are not used more than they are in adult education. Universities and technical colleges have large blackboards, but classes which are held in libraries, museums and village halls present a problem, for it is expected that the 3ft x 3ft[1] (often smaller) blackboards provided will be sufficient. It is at least commonly accepted that science teachers require some kind of blackboard, but it seems to be assumed that the arts and other general subjects require no blackboard at all. Surely, if only for writing down a date or a technical word or giving the correct spelling of a name, a blackboard is a first essential. But blackboard provision of itself is not enough. The blackboard provides an opportunity for initiative, and as blackboard work tends to set an example it should be neat and tidy and requires planned use. Writing should be large and legible—this may seem an elementary point, yet it is astonishing how often it is neglected. The wise use of colour makes illustrations stand out and provides effective emphasis and contrast, and yet coloured chalk is a rare commodity in adult education.

Whatever other aids may be used in a lesson, only rarely can a teacher dispense with a blackboard. A drawback of blackboard work is that drawings have to be done by hand and this may be too slow for interest and attention to be sustained. However, much of this burden can be overcome by the use of cardboard outlines of geometrical shapes, maps and apparatus. Also, when a very complex drawing is necessary, the teacher can draw the diagram before the lesson begins in fine, barely visible lines and then fill these in boldly during the lesson. The 'pattern technique' is also suitable for map drawing. An outline is perforated at intervals by a leather worker's punch. The pattern is then held against the blackboard and a dusty eraser rubbed firmly

across the perforated outlines. The outline of chalk dots so formed is
joined up by hand.

Strictly speaking, one should refer to the conventional blackboard
as a 'chalkboard', for there are many other boards commercially available now which eliminate the problem of chalk and dust. E. J. Arnold,
for example, produce a white, non-glare surface and a set of eight
coloriter crayons which can be easily erased with a clean dry duster.
Similarly, the Education Supply Association produces non-glare grey
markerboards with colour board writers and a special cleaner. Both
of the above are also available as wall boards which can be fixed
permanently to the walls.

Flannelgraph or Feltboard

A piece of flannel or felt has a hairy surface which, when placed
against a similar surface, remains in position because the fibres
interlock. Thus if cut-outs, pictures, etc are given a backing of flannel
they will stick to a flannel board. Adhesion properties of flannel are
not always reliable and there are other materials which have better
adhesive properties, eg velvet, and research has led to the production
of special synthetic fabrics. The technique allows stories and themes to
be built up in front of the class and it can be used in a variety of
subjects. Complete flannelgraph outfits, which comprise letters, words,
maps and products, can be cut out of magazines, or drawings can be
made on stiff paper, and these can be backed with strips of flannel or
sandpaper. In Britain flannelgraphs are mostly used with children, but
in under-developed countries they serve a useful purpose, for example
in teaching health education to illiterate adults.

Magnetic Boards

These work on the same principle as the flannelgraph, are more
expensive, but are more effective as adhesion is better. They can be
made by screwing a sheet of unmagnetised mild steel, painted with
a matt-oil-based spray, to plywood and taping small magnets to card
cut-outs so that the card is held in place on the board. The symbols
and pieces can slide over the board and do not need to be removed.
While this method is applicable to a wide variety of subjects, it is
specially useful for geography and military history. The magnets can
be used to hold charts firmly in position and are better for this purpose
than drawing pins. Small, flat, coloured magnets can also be used as
counters for planning exercises. The painted surface (black is better
than white as the latter reflects glare) can also take white and coloured
chalk, so the board acts in the double capacity of chalkboard and
magnetic board.

Plastigraphs

These are made from thin, smooth, plastic sheeting which remains in position on a flat glossy surface such as glass or plastic board. Letters and shapes cut out of this sheeting are limp and they must be smoothed on to the surface. They are not ideally suited to the rapid development of themes and stories, but are useful for such purposes as bulletin boards. Also, coloured cut-outs can be used for planning factories, kitchens and cookery displays and several layers can be used to illustrate, for example, a section through a biological specimen.

PROJECTORS

The Episcope (or Opaque Projector)

This instrument projects the image of a solid (or opaque) object. Bright light is concentrated on the object (eg a page of a book) and the image is reflected by a mirror through a large lens on to a screen.

The episcope enables objects such as books, maps, pictures and three-dimensional models to show up as large clear images on a screen. But it is a fairly cumbersome piece of equipment and not really portable. Also it produces a great concentration of heat which may destroy flimsy material. Episcopes project objects of up to 10in square, producing sharp colour images measuring 13ft x 13ft. Because only the reflected light is used to illuminate the screen the system is rather inefficient and a complete blackout is necessary.

The projector can project a picture from a magazine or a map on to a blackboard and the outline of the figure can be drawn in with white chalk.

The Epidiascope

The epidiascope combines the functions of an episcope and a diascope; the latter by means of a lens system concentrates or condenses light which is then passed through a slide transparency and focused on to a screen. An epidiascope is a machine which projects lantern slides, ie 3¼in x 3¼in slides. By the addition of a supplementary optical system the episcope becomes an epidiascope. Other attachments can be added to the epidiascope for projecting filmstrips and 2in x 2in slides. But these may cost as much as a separate projector which can perform the same function with greater efficiency.

In America slides are 3¼in x 4½in and on the Continent 9cm x

12cm. Like the episcope, the epidiascope is a rather bulky piece of equipment.

The Microprojector

This shows on the class screen what a single pupil would normally see in a microscope. It has the advantage over the microscope in that all students see the same thing and it eliminates the need for expensive microscopes. It is very versatile and can show tissue cross-sections, bacteria and close-up of cloth fibres.

The Slide Projector (or Diascope)

The most commonly used instrument in education is the miniature diascope or slide projector. This shows 2in x 2in slides or 35mm filmstrip. The pictures may be printed across the film or along the film. The first is termed a single-frame filmstrip and most educational work employs this kind of filmstrip. The second is called a double-frame filmstrip.

The less expensive projectors show one slide at a time in the older 'slide-across' holder or the chute type into which the slides drop. With automatic projectors slides are stacked in straight magazines, 36 at a time in 2in-square mounts, or in circular magazines containing up to 120 slides. These have push-button or other devices which allow the slides to be advanced, and a remote control focusing device. It is advisable to mark the slides clearly so that they are inserted the right way up and in the correct order. When not in use slides can be contained in view packs which allow convenient inspection and handling without damage. Slides are more effective when in colour, but should not contain too much compressed information. The text and diagrams should be large and clearly visible from the back of the classroom. Clarity, simplicity and visual impact should always be aimed at.

Filmstrip carriers may be either of the scroll type or sprocket-operated. All carriers have glass pressure plates between which the film is held while each frame is projected. The sprocket-operated carrier has teeth which engage the sprocket holes and draw it through the pressure plates. These open automatically to prevent scratching of the film. There is usually incorporated a device for 'framing' the film, and thereafter a single twist or flick of the operating knob moves the film on to the next frame. It is important to see that the sprockets of the projector are correctly engaging the sprocket holes in the film, otherwise the film can be damaged.

With the scroll-operated carrier one end of the film is clipped on to a roller and the film fully wound on to it. The free end is passed through the glass slides and fastened to a similar roller. The empty roller is rotated and the film is drawn through the glass pressure plates. This kind of carrier has no framing device, the teacher has to watch the screen while turning on to each new frame. At the same time he has to open the pressure plates to avoid scratching the film and plates. It is essential to perform this latter operation, as the pressure plate is permanent and can only be rectified by replacement of the glasses.

With both filmstrips and slides the teacher must prepare himself and the class and the equipment must be checked in advance. An effective follow-up is also necessary, and this can take the form of a discussion or a test followed by another showing.

There are obviously occasions when sound or music may be necessary as a background or as an essential part of slide presentation. The simplest method of achieving this is to record the proposed track on tape while projecting the slides at a suitable rate, preferably using a magazine projector with remote control. The recorded commentary can have cues in the appropriate places. For more elaborate and sophisticated presentation a special device can be fitted to the recorder. This works on the principle of impulses recorded on the tape. These are applied to, and on replay picked up from, the second track of the tape. The same procedures can be adopted for filmstrip projection. Many such filmstrips are now available.

Slide and filmstrip projectors must have sufficient power, which for a normal classroom is 750-1000 watts. In addition to the power of the lamp the quality of the lenses and reflectors is important in obtaining a brilliant image.

The Overhead Projector

This is a variation of the episcope principle which has the advantage that with only one 500-watt lamp it gives sufficient brilliance of illumination to be used in full daylight. A curved reflector diverts the light from the lamp through the glass table and hence via a mirror through the objective lens which is used for focusing. This has been a most significant advance in the field of still projection, for it can be used without blackout and in addition it enables the teacher to face the class, the screen being behind him.

It can project transparent objects of up to 10in x 10in such as maps, illustrations from books, mechanical drawings and architectural drawings. The term 'transparency' is frequently used for 7in × 7in and 10in × 10in sizes with the overhead projector. The instrument presents great scope for flexibility, and the teacher can make his own transparencies from any original; these may be typed reports, graphs and charts or newspaper clippings. The original and a blank transparency sheet is run through transparency copies. The process takes only seconds to perform and is inexpensive, any number of transparencies being run off in rapid succession.

The overhead projector has the further advantage that the teacher can use the instrument as a substitute for a blackboard—indeed it is far more effective than a blackboard as the contrast is greater and the teacher faces the class as he writes. The writing is done with a china-graph pencil on transparent cellophane paper; a roll of this paper is contained in a holder and as the writing proceeds the paper is drawn across the transparency table. The cellophane can be cleaned with a damp cloth and used again. Prepared transparencies lend themselves to great flexibility and adaptability. For example, if the transparency is a list of points, each of which the teacher needs to impress on the students, these can be hidden from view by a sheet of opaque paper and the points revealed in turn as the teacher deals with them. In dealing with maps use can be made of overlays; the basic transparency can be made to represent the outlines or boundaries of a country and other transparencies illustrating the position of mountains, rivers, cities or basic industries can be placed over the original. The same technique can be used to illustrate battles, physiological processes or complicated machinery. If there are not too many overlays they can be attached to the sides of the projector with sellotape and flicked over as required. Use, too, can be made of the silhouette of objects, for example, leaves in biology. Another convenient device is that of a stacking arrangement of overlays in parallel planes so that separate aspects of a problem can be faded in or out by focusing on a different plane.

The glass plate of the projector must be kept free of dust and finger-marks, and for this purpose it can be wiped with soft cloth damped in lukewarm detergent water. The bulb of the overhead pro-jector has a life expectancy of seventy-five hours, and in any case great care must be exercised; it must not be bumped or jarred as the fila-ment is easily damaged.

Sets of transparencies are now available commercially (a few examples of sources of this material are given below). These consist of some twenty to thirty transparency originals covering some specific topic or subject, and any number of copies can be made from them. They cover a wide variety of subjects, and a set of twenty costs in the region of £10 or so.

Overhead projectors are now available in portable form. They have collapsible heads which allow them to be neatly packed into a compact carrying case. The projector can be used on any desk or table, a simple spring catch engaging when the head arm is raised into position.

SCREENS

There are several different surfaces: beaded, silver, and matt white; each has particular advantages but none has an overall advantage over all the others.

For narrow angle viewing (ie near the projector if this is in the centre of the room) perlux and lenticulated surfaces are better than matt white, but at wider angles the brilliance falls off less rapidly with matt screens and with other surfaces the projectionist may not be aware of this loss of brilliance, Perlux and silver also present creasing problems.

The Film

The film is a clear celluloid ribbon, shiny on one side and dull on the other. The dull side carries a translucent emulsion which holds a visual image or series of images (framed). Down one edge is a row of perforations or sprocket holes into which teeth engage and advance the film. The sound track is a pattern running down the edge of the film.

Cine films come in three sizes: 35mm, 16mm, and 8mm. The 35mm is hardly ever used for teaching; it is the 16mm which is widely accepted for educational purposes. These show respectively 16, 40 and 80 frames to the foot. Standard lengths of these (known as reels) run for 16$\frac{2}{3}$ minutes at 16ft per second and are 1000ft, 400ft and 200ft respectively. In 1965 a further development was the introduction of the Super 8 film. The sprocket holes in this film are of smaller size, which gives an increase in picture area of some 50 per cent. The Super 8 cannot be used on existing 8mm projectors, but convertible dual projectors are becoming available.

The film is probably the closest and most exciting approach to reality. It is the perfect medium for industrial processes and methods. With the use of caricature and animation it becomes possible to translate abstract scientific theories into visual, meaningful terms. The film gives full opportunity for the presentation of performances by the expert and specialist and the sound provides atmosphere where desirable. Use of film has been shown to lead to increased student interest and pupils learn more and retain information better. But, as with other aids, learning is more efficient if both pre-planning and follow-up studies are used.

Many educational institutions make their own films, but a wide variety of films on most subjects can be hired or borrowed from a number of sources. In this respect the magazine *Film User* is useful; it reviews new films, publishes a survey of distributors and provides several hundred names and addresses from which films can be borrowed or hired. These comprise commercial film libraries which charge so much per reel per night; film libraries provided from public funds such as those run by the local educational authorities which serve schools and other educational institutions, and sponsored film libraries. Some examples of film libraries are given in the appendix.

Film Loops or Single Concept Films

These are 8mm, projected on to a screen by special projectors. Their great advantage is that they can be viewed in daylight and require no blackout. Further, no winching or threading is required, the film being contained in a cassette; the cassette is simply inserted into its space, and the projector switched on.

The films are termed 'single concept' because they run for only about five minutes and deal with a single theme or topic. However, the film can be played continuously with unlimited repetition without rewinding or even stopping the projector. Because of the high magnification and the positioning of the camera, the image on the screen (19in × 15in) gives a much clearer picture to a larger number of pupils than can be obtained by demonstration at close range, there being no distortion at the edges and the picture being clearly visible from every angle so that every student sees every demonstration clearly. The film can be stopped and the picture retained at any frame, and on the 20in 'stop-frame' remote-control lead a constant focus is maintained. To eject the cassette the lever at the rear is pressed and the cassette springs out.

Most film-loops currently available are of Standard 8mm, but Super 8 are now on the market. For Standard 8 the film and projectors are cheaper and a wider choice of titles is possible. Super 8 films and projectors are more expensive, but provide somewhat better quality pictures.

CLOSED-CIRCUIT TELEVISION

In closed-circuit television (or CCTV) the signal is received by specific private receivers only, either by transmitting a narrow beam of radiation to specially-directed receiving systems or by linking the camera to the receiver by means of a cable.

CCTV can be used simply as an audio-visual aid to magnify an object, experiment or demonstration. It acts as a microscope which is perfectly adjusted. The camera can be put in places where groups of students cannot be accommodated. Thus it can relay an operation from the operating theatre to monitors housed in a lecture theatre elsewhere in the building, and these can be viewed by a large group of students. All ten of the operating theatres in the new teaching hospital at Liverpool will be fitted up in this way. Again, bedside interviews can be studied by

I

observers on monitors in lecture theatres and reduce the number of occasions on which groups of students have to be taught at the bedside. Another facility offered by CCTV is the storage of information, for the video-tape recorder records sound and vision just as the tape recorder records sound. It is an ideal technique for the training of skills, and is already being used in teacher-training courses. The facilities of the Hull University television studio were used in the training courses run by the University's Extra-Mural Department; sample lessons by the students were taped and then reshown and discussed by the group.[2] One conclusion of this experiment was that in CCTV the spotlight was on the performer and the camera acted like a magnifying glass. Another was that a presentation of a lesson in this way required controlled and precise scripting.

In colleges of education the use of television will revolutionise student observation of teaching methods. Cameras can be installed in the teaching room and pictures transmitted by cable to monitors in another room. Alternatively, the school can be linked by cable to the college of education. Under this system the best teachers can be used as models and the whole group of students share the same experiences with the lecturer and so the discussion can be based on common ground. In the United States observation of the student as a teacher is termed 'microteaching'; a student teaches for five to ten minutes in front of the camera, and his performance is recorded on video-tape. The student then studies his tape and receives an evaluation of his lesson from the other students and from his supervisor.

Video-tape recordings can also be made of prepared lessons and in the preparation of such a lesson slides, charts and models etc can all be brought in and integrated into a stimulating and coherent whole. A recorded lesson has the advantage that modifications can be made by erasing parts of the original tape and re-editing it. Such a lesson requires a great deal of preliminary work, but is justified if it is shown to a large body of students or is repeatedly shown to different groups; in the latter case the material can be continually brought up-to-date over the years. In a televised course of physics for engineering students at Brunel University it was calculated that a thirty-five minute video-tape required twenty hours of the time of the lecturer and producer. Students were given printed summaries before each lecture so that they could concentrate on the lecture. It was found that the presentation was smoother than that of a normal lecture, and complicated diagrams and equations could be prepared in advance and not written out laboriously in front of the students. It was estimated that a normal hour's lecture could be put across by this method in thirty-five minutes and the time saved could be spent on seminar or tutorial work.

About six local education authorities in Britain are now operating or thinking of operating closed circuit systems to cover schools and colleges. The first full-time local authority system to work on a regular daily schedule was Glasgow ETV (Educational Television). This came into operation in 1965 and it links over 300 schools and further education colleges in the area to the central studio. The main emphasis at Glasgow had been on spoken French for the primary schools and modern mathematics for the first year of the secondary schools, and the programmes have been scripted and presented by practising teachers of the city. The Inner London Educational Authority is planning a very ambitious network which will come into operation in 1970; the transmission will reach a thousand schools, schools of art, technical colleges and colleges of commerce at a cost of about £150 per school or college per year. London, like Glasgow, is going to produce its system in consultation with teachers, and the programmes will also be presented by teachers.

Local area television offers advantages and resources not available to the single teacher or school. For example, it is common practice in day-release work for teachers to repeat identical lessons and demonstrations on several days of the week. Each lesson can be recorded on video-tape and shown on many further occasions. Again, local television offers a variety of resources such as the presentation of skilled specialists or experts, skilled graphic work, animated cartoons by specialist artists and so on.

ELECTRONIC VIDEO-RECORDING

Very shortly a revolutionary new technique will be coming on to the market. Known as electronic video-recording, this will provide the visual equivalent of the long-playing record.

Visual material is recorded on to microfilm which is then viewed by electronic scanning as in television, rather than by normal projection. The 8.75mm film contains a series of images one-tenth the size of those on the normal 16mm conventional cine film, but they are of much better quality. The film will contain two tracks—90,000 frames on each—which will provide one hour of playing time. The operating procedure is very simple, in the form of a $7in \times \frac{1}{2}in$ diameter cassette film cartridge. It is inserted into a EVR teleplayer (estimated to cost £200) which is connected to the aerial socket of a normal domestic television receiver. It is possible to link the player to several receivers simultaneously. The operator will be able to control the film so that a slow scan of frames is attained or it can be stopped and restarted.

The film cartridges will be a translation of conventional 16mm films so it will mean that copies of films and plays presented by the BBC, independent networks and other bodies will become available commercially and can be played on an EVR teleplayer in the same way as long-playing records are now played on gramophones. EVR is likely to be of value in three main educational fields: secondary distribution of schools' programmes already broadcast; providing for schools in outlying areas those services which the big-city CCTV systems are already providing in their own areas; and providing for the distribution of the TV element in the Open University teaching programme.

THE TAPE RECORDER

Some students who do not respond readily to visual stimuli may learn more quickly from sound stimuli. But in using aural methods care must be taken to discover whether any students have imperfections in hearing; at least five per cent of the school population and probably far more adults have such imperfections.

The main aural aid is the tape recorder, which can teach single students, small groups and large numbers. The range of subject matter available on tape is extensive—it covers speech and language training, music, drama, social studies—and the tape recorder has relevance to nearly every subject. Like the video-tape recorder it lends itself to evaluation and assessment through its playback facility and recorded tapes.

Since the end of World War II a revolution has taken place in the approach to language teaching, in which the aim has been to teach a language not as a means of understanding the literature of a country but in order that the student may be able to communicate in its language. The term 'direct method' is generally understood to apply to the means of achieving this. The basis of it is that, instead of learning formal grammar and pronunciation in the usual way, the students learn in the same manner as they learned their own language, ie aurally and not by the written word.

The tape recorder makes use of magnetic tapes which are thin, plastic ribbons a quarter of an inch wide. One side is dull, and this is coated with a magnetic slide of iron on which the recording is made.

Recorders produced since 1959 have halved the tracks once more and the tape is thus used for four tracks. This has meant that the playing time has quadrupled, but with such narrow tracks particles of dust will lift the head away from the tape and cause distortion of sound; hence it is essential to keep tapes free of dust.

The playing time of the tape is increased by using only half the width of the track, for when the tape has reached the end of its run in one direction (using the top half or track) it is inverted and run through again using the other half.

Tapes come in different lengths. As recordings can be made at different speeds, tapes have a variety of playing times. These are shown below. The introduction of 'long-play' tapes makes it possible to increase the playing time of standard tapes by 50 per cent.

Tape Running Times

Reel Size	Tape Length	Speed	Running Time	
			One Track	Both Tracks
3-in standard	300ft	$1\frac{7}{8}$ips	$\frac{1}{2}$hr	1hr
		$3\frac{3}{4}$ips	$\frac{1}{4}$hr	$\frac{1}{2}$hr
		$7\frac{1}{2}$ips	$7\frac{1}{2}$mins	$\frac{1}{4}$hr
5-in standard	600ft	$1\frac{7}{8}$ips	1hr	2hr
		$3\frac{3}{4}$ips	$\frac{1}{2}$hr	1hr
		$7\frac{1}{2}$ips	$\frac{1}{4}$hr	$\frac{1}{2}$hr
7-in standard	1,200ft	$1\frac{7}{8}$ips	2hr	4hr
		$3\frac{3}{4}$ips	1hr	2hr
		$7\frac{1}{2}$ips	$\frac{1}{2}$hr	1hr

Generally speaking the faster the speed the better the quality of sound, but usually the slowest speed is used to record speech.

THE RECORD PLAYER

This played an important part in the early development of language laboratories, and even today a number of them include gramophone as well as tape facilities. But the gramophone has great usefulness in the learning of languages at home and a number of 'teach yourself' records are available. In addition, the gramophone is widely used for a variety of purposes which include musical appreciation, poetry readings and drama, music and movement, dancing and song, and an increasing amount of educational material is becoming available on disc.

THE MULTI-MEDIA APPROACH

This is the bringing together and integration of different techniques and media to teach a given programme. A number of multi-media instructional laboratories have been set up in the United States. A typical one contains slide projectors, film projectors, tape recorders, overhead projectors and other equipment, all of which can be controlled from the teacher's console and quickly brought into action when required by the flick of a switch. Visual material can be presented simultaneously on several screens in alliance with music or a tape recording. As in the language laboratory, the teacher is in direct communication with each individual student, who has an array of buttons at his disposal. The teacher may ask questions during the lecture and may suggest alternative answers, the student pressing the appropriate button for a correct answer. The proportion of students in the class giving different responses is indicated on the teacher's console. As a result he is able to adapt the pace and level of his lecture to the needs of the majority of students.

Appendix

COMMERCIAL TRANSPARENCIES

Filipatran,
Transart Ltd,
Visual Education Department,
East Chadley Lane,
Godmanchester,
Huntingdon.

Educational Supply Association,
Schools Material Division,
Pinnacles,
Harlow,
Essex.

Macmillan & Co Ltd,
Little Essex St,
London W.C 2.

3M Minnesota Mining and Manu-
facturing Company Ltd,
Head Office, 3M House,
Wigmore Street,
PO Box 1ET,
London W1.

FILMS

The National Film Library operated by the British Film Institute.
The National Audio-Visual Aids Library,
Paxton Place, Gipsy Road, London SE 27.

The Foundation Film Library,
Brooklands House, Weybridge, Surrey.

This is the national library of educational films for England and Wales and holds a wide range of 16mm films, 35mm filmstrips and 2in × 2in slides.

Catalogues available from
The Educational Foundation for Visual Aids,
33 Queen Anne Street, London W.7.

For hire of 16mm film copies of selected BBC programmes,
Brian Keyer,
Education and Training Film Sales,
BBC TV Enterprises, Haven Green, London W5.

Sound Services Ltd,
Kingston Road, Merton Park, London SW19.
   Has a large sponsored library with 2,000 titles, the majority of them on free loan.

Industrial and commercial films and filmstrips can be obtained on free loan from such firms as

Shell Films,
The Petroleum Films Bureau,
4 Brook Street,
Hanover Square,
London W1.

Courtaulds Textiles Films
from
Sound Services Film Library.

BP Films,
Audi-Pix Ltd,
48a Goodge Street,
London EC1.

OVERHEAD PROJECTORS

Name of Projector, Distributor, Country and Cost
ICEM, Macmillan & Co, Britain, Standard 8, £88.50, Super 8 not yet available.
THD, Sound Services Ltd, Britain, Standard 8 £87.50, Super 8 £91.50.
Technicolour 600, Rank Audio-Visual Ltd, USA, Standard 8 £131.25.
Technicolour 610, USA, Super 8 £230.
Standard 8mm loops cost £2-3.

FILM LOOPS

Sound Services Ltd,
Kingston Road, London SW19.
   Provide over 900 titles.

Ealing Scientific Limited,
23, Leman Street, London E1.
   600 titles on a wide variety of topics. Ealing provide a film loop

directory listing all titles of film loops produced in the United Kingdom and also a leaflet on film loop projectors and accessories, listing all projectors and accessories.

Macmillan & Co Ltd,
   600 titles in Standard 8 or Super 8. Orders and requests for inspection copies (up to 14 days).
Inspection Copy Service,
Macmillan and Co Ltd,
Brunel Road, Basingstoke.

The Foundation Film Library,
Brooklands House, Weybridge, Surrey.

USEFUL ADDRESSES

National Committee for Audio-
  Visual Aids in Education,
33 Queen Anne Street,
London W1.

Educational Foundation for
  Visual Aids,
33 Queen Anne Street,
London W1.

National Audio-Visual Aids
  Centre,
Paxton Place,
Gypsy Road,
London SE27.

Oversea Visual-Aids Centre,
31 Tavistock Square,
London WC1.

Nuffield Foundation,
Tavistock House South,
Tavistock Square,
London WC1.

Association for Programmed
  Learning and Educational
  Technology,
27 Torrington Square,
London WC1.

Rank Audio-Visual,
Woodger's Road,
Shepherd's Bush,
London W12.

The Central Film Library,
Government Building,
Bramyard Avenue,
London W3.

Foundation Film Library,
Brooklands House,
Weybridge,
Surrey.

Film User,
PO Box 109,
Croydon,
Surrey.

Centre for Information on Language Teaching,
State House,
High Holborn,
London WC1.

The OVAC Bulletin,
Oversea Visual Aids Centre,
31 Tavistock Square,
London WC1.

Audio-Visual Communication
  Review,
Department of Audio-Visual
  Instruction,
1207 16th Street, NW,
Washington DC,
USA.

Visual Education,
33 Queen Anne Street,
London W1.

Educational Technology,
Educational News Service,
PO Box 508, Saddle Brook,
New Jersey,
USA.

NOTES

1   Wittich, W. A. and Schuller, C. E. *Audio-Visual Materials* (New York 1967) advocate 20 linear feet of blackboard
2   Styler, W. E. 'Training Through Television', *Adult Education,* 41 no 5 (1969)

FURTHER READING

Atkinson, N. J. *Modern Teaching Aids* (1966)
Dale, E. *Audio-Visual Methods* (New York 1965)
Harding, D. H. *The New Pattern of Language Teaching* (1967)
Lamb, R. T. B. *The Aids to Modern Teaching: a Short Survey* (1967)
Lowe, M. and Lowe, J. (eds). *On Teaching Foreign Languages to Adults* (Oxford 1965)
Mathieu, G. (ed). *Advances in the Teaching of Modern Languages* vol 2 (Oxford 1967)
Shaplin, J. T. and Olds, J. H. F. *Team Teaching* (New York 1964)
Stack, E. M. *The Language Laboratory and Modern Language Teaching* (New York 1966)
Anwin, D. and Leedham, J. (eds). *Aspects of Educational Technology* (1967)
Cable, R. *Audio-Visual Handbook* (1965)
Milner, C. D. *Making Lantern Slides and Filmstrips* (1957)
Wittich, W. A. *Audio-Visual Materials; their Nature and Use* (New York 1967)
Maclean, R. *Television in Education* (1968)

11 The Principles of Programmed Learning

Geoffrey Leytham

When the writer recently asked a group of teachers in adult education what sort of thing they associated with programmed learning, their replies were revealing and helpful, if somewhat disconcerting. Machines and pigeons were mentioned several times, and one got the general impression that programmed learning was regarded as an inhuman, mechanistic process, with little relevance to adult education. It is most unfortunate that many teachers associate programmed learning solely with teaching machines, which they sometimes see as a threat to their livelihood. In fact, the aims of the *principles* of programmed learning are just the opposite; where machines are used their purpose is to relieve the teacher of routine and tedious instruction so that he has more time to teach. Far from supplanting the teacher, programmed learning seeks to help him to make the most of his abilities and aptitudes. It also stresses the importance of the individual student, whose uniqueness and dignity it acknowledges and respects.

Historically the term 'programmed learning' derives from an article by the American psychologist B. F. Skinner, published in 1954 and entitled: 'The Science of Learning and the Art of Teaching'. Admittedly much of the science of learning is based on research using animals and birds, including pigeons, but the whole purpose of Skinner's article was to indicate how these research findings could be applied to the practice of teaching. To the extent that teaching machines embody the principles of programmed learning they are relevant to our discussion, but the use of them is controlled by the teacher. The art of teaching, in common with other arts, involves the selection of the right techniques and aids to achieve a desired objective. Programmed learning is primarily concerned with objectives and general principles of procedure, a consideration of which must obviously precede any concern with particular methods of application.

The principles of programmed learning are largely common sense, and good teachers tend to follow them automatically. However, it may be as well to list these principles before dealing with each one separately.

The aims and objectives of a course of learning should be clearly and explicitly specified in advance in terms of observable behaviour.

The material to be learned should be selected with reference to the aims and objectives of the course of learning.

It should be organised in short, progressive steps, following a logical sequence.

It should be graded in difficulty so that the student makes few mistakes as he proceeds.

Each student should be introduced to new material at a level of difficulty commensurate with his past experience and current attainments.

Each student should proceed through the course of learning at his own pace.

He should be actively involved in the process of learning.

He should receive continual knowledge of how he is progressing through the course of learning.

He should master each section of the material before continuing with the next.

These general principles can be applied to almost all aspects of education, on any time-scale, but the emphasis in the following discussion will be placed on their application to the teaching of adults. The teacher's main function is to consider their relevance to his own particular subject.

In discussing the application of the principles of programmed learning to a specific course, one encounters a problem which is crucial in all aspects of formal education. This is the problem of what is technically known as 'transfer'. In everyday language this concerns the extent to which past learning can be applied to new situations. In a recent research investigation, for instance, it was found that there was no measurable transfer from a course on educational psychology to teaching in the classroom. In other words, there was no correlation between marks obtained on the course examination and grades allocated for teaching practice. In the same way it would be quite possible for a person training to be a teacher to memorise all the principles of programmed learning and to pass an examination on them without this having any notice-

able effect on his teaching. This may be because the relevance of prior
learning is not appreciated in a subsequent practical situation, or because
learning is directed at passing examinations, which are regarded as ends
in themselves. In either case the teacher can help by relating the material
learned to the sort of situation for which it is intended. To do this
it is obviously necessary to define and analyse the aims and objectives
of the course concerned, even if it does not seem to have any obvious
practical implications. The aims and objectives of a course on car maintenance, for instance, would be easier to define than those of one on
English literature. This raises two general educational problems which
should be considered before dealing with more specific matters. The
two problems are closely related, one being concerned with the type
of course taught and the other with the kind of learning experienced by
the student.

When the economics of adult education are being considered, frequent
use is made of the terms 'vocational' and 'non-vocational', there being a
tendency to regard the former type of course as more worthy of financial
support than the latter. However, I entirely agree with Professor Kelly's
views, as expressed in his inaugural lecture 'Adult Education at the
Cross Roads' (1969).[1] He feels that 'to those familiar with what
actually goes on in adult education the terms "vocational" and "non-
vocational" often seem curiously irrelevant'. He cites a course on the
ethical issues involved in some recent advances in medicine, and asks
whether those who attended this course did so out of purely vocational
interest (many of them were doctors and social workers) or whether 'they
were motivated alike by professional interest and by a deep concern
as human beings?' In conclusion, he expresses the opinion that 'there
are no such things as vocational and non-vocational subjects; there are
only vocational and non-vocational students, and they are frequently to
be found in the same class.'

The other problem, which also involves the individual student, concerns a distinction which Maslow has made between extrinsic and intrinsic learning. In a talk given at Esalen Institute, California in 1966, he
discussed 'the goals of humanistic education' and expressed the opinion
that most educators concentrated on extrinsic learning to the detriment
of the intrinsic kind. Maslow defined extrinsic learning as 'essentially
an acquisition of something which is not of the personality'. It is concerned mainly with learning facts and with acquiring the sorts of knowledge which do not change an individual in any fundamental way. Intrinsic learning, on the other hand, is more concerned with human growth
and development and helps a person to progress towards maturity. Just
as it would be wrong to divide courses into vocational and non-vocational, so it would be misleading to relate practical courses to extrinsic

learning and liberal studies to intrinsic learning. Education, as the word implies, involves the drawing out and development of individual potentialities as well as the provision of instruction in facts and techniques. The teacher seeks to help and guide individual students; hence the art of teaching embraces both kinds of learning.

With the above discussion in mind, it is now possible to turn to a more detailed consideration of each of the principles of programmed learning enumerated on page 140. These will be dealt with from the point of view of the teacher who is preparing a particular course of study.

The aims and objectives of a course of learning should be clearly and explicitly specified in advance in terms of observable behaviour

Mager[2] distinguishes between the description of a course and its objectives. The former indicates what the course is about (often the title), while the latter specifies what a successful student should be able to do at the end of the course. Many teachers have little or no control over the description of the course which they are asked to teach, but in selecting and organising its content they would obviously find it helpful to decide beforehand what changes and modifications they hope to bring about in the students who attend. To do this it is necessary to specify the objectives fairly explicitly. What practical things should the student be able to do by the end of the course? Which techniques should he have acquired? What factual questions should he be able to answer? Should he be able to make certain discriminations as a result of taking the course? Will any personal characteristics of the student be affected? Further pertinent questions might be suggested by referring to the outline of the seven-point plan, which is given later (page 144). With questions such as these in mind, it should be possible to define the aims and objectives of the course in terms of *observable* behaviour, and not in abstract terms such as 'to understand' 'to know', 'to have a good grasp of', etc. These terms are quite acceptable in course descriptions intended for prospectuses, but in preparing his material the teacher should decide beforehand how the student will be required to *demonstrate* his understanding and knowledge. In short, and using the concept in its widest sense, it is necessary to consider the final examination *before* starting to select and organise the content of a course.

Such an explicit definition of the objectives of a course is referred to in programmed learning language as 'criterion behaviour'. However, this not only involves a specification of the behaviour expected from the student on completion of the course, but also a statement as to the level of achievement that he should reach. It would not, for instance, be sufficient to define the objectives of a course in typing as 'the ability to use a typewriter'. It would be necessary to specify the speed and accuracy with which given material should be typed on completion of the course in order to pass. In this way, the competence of the typist can be assessed, with reference to measurable performance.

At the end of Mager's book there is a test to assess the reader's ability to identify observable behaviour and to recognise a criterion of acceptable performance. Fourteen statements of course objectives are given, and for each one the reader has to decide whether either or both the requirements are given. One could therefore use this test for a course on the principles of programmed learning. One objective of such a course could be stated as 'The student should be able to complete Mager's test and to get at least 80 per cent of his answers correct.'

While the aims and objectives of specific courses may be relatively easy to state and evaluate, the more general aims of certain educational procedures do not so readily lend themselves to definition. However, as general claims are frequently made about particular forms of education, often implying 'transfer' to a broad range of activities, it is essential that the criterion behaviour be specified in order to test whether the claims are substantiated.

The onus is now on the teacher to demonstrate just what a student does gain from attending his course. He will be in a much better position to do this if his aims and objectives are clearly defined and open to evaluation.

The material to be learned should be selected with reference to the aims and objectives of the course of learning.

Learning obviously involves change and modification in the individual student, and it might be helpful to think of it as a process of enrichment. This would include both a wider and more comprehensive knowledge through extrinsic learning and also enrichment of the person himself through intrinsic learning. There are few tasks which have no psychological component, and it is interesting to note that in a study of airline pilots the crucial factor which distinguished the best ones from the poorer was a personality characteristic. Similarly, investigations of road accidents suggest that psychological factors are more important than technical ones in accounting for accidents. A person may handle a car with great skill, but if he is aggressive on the road and inconsiderate of others one would hesitate to call him a good driver.

In deciding what sort of material is relevant to the aims and objectives of a course, it is helpful to analyse the specified criterion behaviour in terms of the various abilities and qualities required to achieve it. This is usually referred to as 'task analysis' and involves not only a description of the characteristics essential for mastering the task but also an understanding of how all the facets are interrelated and the relative importance of each.

In making such a task analysis the teacher will find that the seven-point plan proposed by Rodger ('Symposium on the selection of pupils for different types of secondary school—viii. An industrial psychologist's point of view'), British Journal of Educational Psychology, 19 (1949) pp 154-9, provides a useful framework. Full details, together with the twenty-six questions relating to the plan, are given in the article. A brief summary follows:

Physical Characteristics: Does the task involve any special physical attributes in the learner, and are his appearance, bearing and speech of any importance?

Attainments and Previous Experience: Does the task require any special kind of educational or occupational training and experience?

General Intelligence: What minimum level of intelligence does the task require?

Special Aptitudes: Does the task require an aptitude for understanding mechanical things, manual dexterity, fluent expression in speech or writing, a flair for mathematics, an ability to draw well, or a musical talent?

Interests: What sorts of interest are relevant to the task: intellectual, practical-constructional, physically-active, social or artistic?

Personality: How far do temperament and other psychological factors influence the way in which the task is carried out?

Social: Are social background and experience related to competence in the task?

An illuminating task analysis, and one of great interest would be that produced by a teacher whose course is concerned with the training of teachers!

Once the task analysis has been carried out, the teacher should be in a position to select and order his material and to classify it in order of importance. In doing this, he might find the following three categories helpful:

Essential: material that the student *must* know to achieve the course objectives.

Desirable: material which *should* be known but is not essential.
Useful: material that *could* be known but is not so important for the immediate aims of the course.

The need for such a classification will become more apparent when we discuss the individual student, who is the learner and for whom the course is prepared. Naturally the teacher's objective is to enable each individual student to attain the criterion behaviour specified for his course.

The material to be learned should be organised in short, progressive steps, following a logical sequence.

Having collected a pool of material as a result of his task analysis, the teacher's next step is to decide on the best sequence of presentation. It should be stressed at this point that, while the principles of programmed learning have so far been mainly applied to the construction of formal programmes, they are equally applicable to all forms of teaching. The object of this chapter is to encourage teachers to make fuller use of these principles in all aspects of their work.

Whether he wishes to write a formal programme or to organise his course material, the teacher could not do better at this juncture than to study the excellent book *Programmed Learning in Perspective*.[3] Although written mainly to help people to write linear programmes (of which more later), this book contains some most helpful advice for all concerned with organising teaching material. The authors offer the following guidance to help in deciding on the best and most logical sequence to follow. They suggest that the programme or course should proceed from

the known to the unknown;
the simple to the complex;
the concrete to the abstract;
observations to reasoning;
a whole view to a more detailed analysis.

K

There is no space in this short chapter to describe all the stages of organisation given in the book, but briefly the next step is to take the main *concepts* indicated by the task analysis and the criterion behaviour and to put these into a logical sequence. Then it is necessary to derive a series of rules from each concept and to write each rule on a separate card. Each sequence of rules is tested in a matrix and adjustments are made until the best sequence is arrived at. (In writing this chapter, for instance, this advice was invaluable in deciding upon the best order in which to present the principles of programmed learning). It is unlikely that for any given material there will be one perfect pattern, but some sequences are certainly better than others, although not everyone would probably agree as to which was the best. The main aim is to link concepts so that the whole programme or course flows smoothly. With the principles of programmed learning, for example, the endeavour was to relate the aims and objectives to the material, and the material to the student, in a relatively unbroken sequence.

Once the concepts and rules have been organised, it is a fairly simple matter to add examples to each rule and to expand the programme or course internally in the form of frames, exercises, projects, etc. An instance of a concept with a related rule and example, might be:

> Concept: Expansion.
> Rule: Metals expand when heated.
> Example: Telegraph wires sag in hot weather.

Another way of organising material, which combines the principles of programmed learning with those of information theory, is the 'algorithm'. This procedure was introduced by Russian psychologists and consists of an instruction followed by 'if—then' statements. This is also a helpful way of presenting complex arguments in a diagrammatic form. An example is given in the book *Teaching Machines and Programmed Instruction*,[4] where a diagram providing a succession of binary choices is used as a guide for identifying faults in a programme. An algorithm is really an exact recipe which provides a correct and orderly sequence of instructions for answering questions or solving problems.

The material to be learned should be graded in difficulty so that the student makes few mistakes as he proceeds.

Confidence is a most important factor in learning, and the teacher should do all in his power to give the student confidence in his ability to master the material presented in the course. Initial failure is likely to deter the student and make it more difficult for him to learn. It is

thus helpful to build up confidence through success at the very beginning. This provides reinforcement and encouragement and makes the
student more eager to proceed with the next part of the course. To
maximise success and minimise failure, fairly wide tolerance levels
should be used in the early stages of the course. A good example of this
is given in a study by Jamieson,[5] who produced a programme for training
sewing machinists. When the traditional method of training was used,
older women tended to drop out before the course was completed. The
main reason for this was that the accuracy required at the very beginning
of the training was so stringent that they were continually failing to
reach the set standards and hence did not consider themselves suitable
for the job. Jamieson's programme allowed the beginner to sew anywhere along a wide channel, and as her confidence was built up she
sewed along progressively narrower tracks until she was sewing along
a perfectly straight line. Using this method of training, all the older
people successfully mastered the technique and stayed on to continue
the job. Similar results have been obtained in the teaching of statistics,
where symbols have been introduced very gradually, to build up the
student's confidence before introducing more difficult material. Once the
student feels happy about the symbols and his ability to understand and
master them, the learning process can be speeded up and he proceeds
with confidence.

*Each student should be introduced to new material at a level of
difficulty commensurate with his past experience and current attainments.*

In an attempt to apply the principles of programmed learning to the
whole of a one-year course, 'The Psychology of Learning', I constructed
an initial test to find out what the students knew about the subject
already. They were all second-year students reading for honours degrees
in the social sciences, and all had completed an introductory course in
psychology the previous year.

An alphabetical list of the concepts to be covered in the course was
presented to each student, together with a sheet giving the names of
associated psychologists, also arranged in alphabetical order. The task
was to match the names with the concepts and to write them in accordingly. Allowing one point for each correct match, a total score of 175
was possible. The average obtained by a class of thirty-three students
was 24, and the individual scores ranged from 8 to 56.

The test helped the student by being an introduction to the concepts
and names to be covered by the course (whole view), and by giving some

idea of how much was already known. It helped the teacher to ascertain the class's existing knowledge and to decide where each student should start with the material to be presented.

The answers to each item on the test were analysed to find the relative familiarity of each concept. Some were well-known to all members of the class and could be omitted. There seemed little need, for instance, to say much more about Pavlov's salivating dogs and the concept of 'conditioned response'. On the other hand, none of the students had heard of algorithms, while only half the class knew much about the 'law of effect'.

If such diverse knowledge exists among university students taking a course revelant to their full-time degree studies, how much wider will be the gap between older students joining part-time adult classes on a variety of subjects. Nothing is calculated to sap the confidence of a beginner more than to join an introductory class where 'no prior knowledge of the subject is necessary', only to find that everyone else knows a great deal about the topic already. If the teacher allows the better-informed students to set the pace, the real beginner may be lost for ever—not only from that class, but from all others in the future.

Each individual student should proceed through the course of learning at his own pace.

Individual differences (which span the whole range of factors mentioned in the seven-point plan) involve not only diversities in background and experience, but also differences in temperament and ability. Thus it is obvious that not only should a student start a course at a place appropriate to his existing knowledge and skills, but also that he should subsequently proceed at his own speed.

In a course on educational psychology, given to postgraduate students taking the Certificate in Education at Liverpool, the effects of presenting the same material in three different ways were compared. A third of the class attended the usual lectures, another third had lectures which were heavily augmented with audio-visual aids, and the remaining third worked through Stones' programmed text *Learning and Teaching*.[6] The last group studied the nine sections of Stones' book while the other students were attending lectures. A test, specially prepared by Stones, was administered to all students at the beginning and end of the one-term course. It was found that the students using the programmed text scored significantly higher on the post-test than the other two groups, and also showed greater improvement during the interval between pre-test and post-test. When the test was given again after an interval of

six months, this superiority was maintained. Most of the students preferred the programmed procedure, mainly because they could proceed
at their own speed. Their time for each section of the programmed text
varied from less than thirty minutes to an hour. Hence many students
were covering the same material as in the lectures in appreciably less
time and with better retention. In this case, therefore, learning was more
efficient when done at the individual student's own pace.

The student should be actively involved in the process of learning.

When working through a programme presented either in a text-book
or by means of a teaching machine, the student not only determines
the pace at which he shall progress but also actively participates in the
learning procedure. In some types of programme he has to write his
response to a frame before looking at the next one (linear programme),
and in others he has to check the answer he has selected from a
group of possibilities, either by turning to a specific page in a book
or by pressing a given button on the teaching machine (branching
programme).

There is ample evidence to show that active participation and involvement produce better learning than a more passive, detached approach.
A moment's reflection on one's own experiences will confirm this. As
a passenger in a car, one rarely remembers the route as well as the
driver who was actively concerned with finding his way from one place
to another. A student attending a lecture is usually more like a passenger
than a driver as far as active involvement is concerned. In experiments
carried out by McLeish and reported in his book *The Lecture Method*,
it was found that students retained only about 40 per cent of a lecture
immediately afterwards, and that half of that had been forgotten a
week later. This shows, as did our research mentioned in the last
section, how inefficient the lecture is as a method of teaching and
learning.

*The student should receive continual knowledge of how he is progressing
through the course of learning.*

Active involvement facilitates learning better than passive detachment,
but it does not necessarily ensure that the learning is accurate or that
it helps the student to progress towards the criterion behaviour. We all
know, from the bad habits of which we are ashamed, that practice per-
fects faults as well as virtues. If the student is to correct his errors as

he goes along, he must have continual feedback or knowledge of results, and this can best be provided by the teacher.

After several weeks in a French course for beginners, a student was asked to write the French for 'I am' on the board. He walked up, and without hesitation wrote: 'Just we'. Incredible, but true. He had never been asked to write it before, so how could he have known he was wrong? The provision of corrective information is one of the main functions of a teacher. It is, perhaps, the one most neglected, and in adult classes where no written work is required it may be overlooked altogether. If it is, then in this respect the human teacher is certainly inferior to the mechanical one.

As indicated in the last section, formal programmes, whether presented in book form or by means of a teaching machine, require the student to make some response to every frame, and to check that response before continuing with the next. In linear programmes the student writes his response to the frame and immediately uncovers the answer to check whether or not he is correct. In branching programmes, where more information is presented per frame, the student usually has to select an answer from a number of possibilities. Each answer has a corresponding page or frame, to which the student turns or which he has presented to him by pressing the relevant button on the machine. He is informed of the correctness of his answer, and if it is correct the next portion of material is available to him. However, if the student chooses a wrong answer, the nature of his error is indicated on what is called a 'remedial' frame, where a suitable correction is given.

The student should master each section of the material before continuing with the next.

When the student has worked through the remedial frame on a branching programme, he is returned to the original question and must select the right answer before receiving new material. If he makes a further mistake he will find another remedial frame presented to him, followed by the original question again. The programme thus ensures that the student masters each piece of material before proceeding to the next.

Progress is thus built on mastery and gives the student a feeling of achievement and confidence. The criterion behaviour to which the course or programme leads is often psychologically remote, and hence tends to lose much of its motivational force. However, in dividing the programme or course into a large number of sub-goals, a continual sense of urgency is generated, and motivation is maintained as the student checks each response along the way. Encouragement and reward are increased and, in the terminology of learning theory, the student receives continuous 'reinforcement'. This form of continuous assessment not only gives him repeated knowledge of how he is progressing, but also diminishes the anxiety which arises from having a whole year's work assessed in one omnibus examination. In fact, when a student has completed a programme or course based on the principles of programmed learning, there is really no need for a final examination along traditional lines. Having mastered each stage as he proceeded, the student should be in a position to satisfy the criterion behaviour when he has successfully ended the programme or course. The final assessment would therefore cover only the criterion behaviour and not all the steps that led up to it.

If the teacher has been successful in organising his course, the student's 'terminal behaviour' should correspond with the 'criterion behaviour' specified by the teacher at the outset. If the terminal behaviour of an appreciable number of students falls short of the criterion behaviour, then the fault is as much in the teaching as in the learning. The emphasis is thus changed from students passing or failing to courses passing or failing, and it is essential, if education is to progress, that it should be possible to evaluate the efficiency of a course so that it can be modified and improved where necessary. After all, the principles of programmed learning apply as much to the teacher as to the student, for how can he ever improve his teaching if he does not receive continual feedback from each individual student throughout the course? The success and future development of adult education will depend to a large extent upon an increasing insight into the student-teacher relationship. It is hoped that the principles of programmed learning will help to provide such insights, which should not only benefit both the teacher and the taught, but also everyone else with whom they come into contact.

NOTES

1 Kelly, T. *Adult Education at the Cross Roads* (Liverpool 1969)
2 Mager, R. F. *Preparing Instructional Objectives* (Palo Alto, California 1962)
3 Thomas, C. A., Davies, I. K., Openshaw, D. and Bird, J. B. *Programmed Learning in Perspective* (1963)
4 Kay, H., Dodd, B. and Sime, M. *Teaching Machines and Programmed Learning* (1968)

5 Jamieson, G. H. 'Age, Speed and Accuracy: a Study in Industrial Retraining', *Occupational Psychology,* 40 (1966), 237-42

6 Stones, E. *Learning and Teaching: A Programmed Introduction* (1968)

FURTHER READING

See list at end of Chapter 12.

12 Applications of Programmed Learning

Geoffrey Leytham

The principles of programmed learning, enumerated and discussed in the last chapter, can serve many purposes; the aim of this chapter is to indicate some of these.

The list of principles provides a framework for the evaluation of teaching methods. The extent to which any particular method satisfies the nine given principles may be taken as some measure of its efficiency as an aid to learning. Few methods currently in use satisfy all nine requirements and some, like the lecture, hardly seem to meet any of them. There is no reason, of course, why a traditional method such as the lecture should not be improved in the light of such an evaluation. It is possible, for instance, to involve the student more actively by asking questions during the lecture and by making sure that each point has been understood before progressing to the next. Research is currently being conducted into what is called the 'feedback classroom', where a question is asked and a number of possible answers are provided, as in branching programmes. Each student selects the answer which he feels is correct and indicates his choice to the teacher. This can be done by mechanical means or in any other way that assures anonymity. Provided with such feedback, the teacher is able to correct any misapprehensions before continuing. There are, of course, other, more indirect methods of ascertaining the extent to which the group is following a talk or lecture. A sensitive teacher soon becomes aware of blank expressions, signs of restlessness etc.

The principles of programmed learning can act as a framework, not only for evaluating and improving traditional methods of teaching, but also for helping in the selection of appropriate audio-visual aids. If one were to compare education with travelling, then programmed learning would be concerned with destinations and routes, while audio-visual aids would provide the means of transport. A fuller account of the relationship between programmed learning and audio-visual aids at the university level is given in the Brynmor Jones report *Audio-Visual Aids in*

153

Higher Scientific Education (1965), and in an article by the writer in the journal *New University* (1969). It is now fashionable to refer to both these aspects of the learning and teaching process as 'educational technology'. In this book, these two chapters on programmed learning and the preceding one on teaching aids give a fair indication of the scope of this new subject.

Other chapters also include material related to educational technology; hence the principles of programmed learning may even be used as a means of bringing about a synthesis of the different aspects of this book. In at least three chapters, for instance, reference is made to the aims and objectives of adult classes. Some chapters are concerned with the selection and organisation of course material, some refer to student involvement and feedback, several mention individual differences among students, and some consider the relationship between the teacher and the student. Problems involved in the selection and evaluation of teaching methods are also discussed.

Programmed learning is mentioned specifically in Chapter 14 in relation to tuition by correspondence, and teachers in adult education may well feel that this is the sort of situation in which it is most relevant. Helping students with their private studies is certainly one way in which programmed learning can help, and later in this chapter reference will be made to programmed texts and teaching machines, which students can use on their own either at home or in class. At this point, however, I would like to emphasise that the whole purpose of these two chapters on programmed learning is to suggest that the general principles outlined in them are applicable to all aspects of education. The principles of programmed learning should be thought of as central to the whole educational process and not just as adjuncts that may be useful on occasions. Naturally their application requires flexibility and imagination, and those trained in traditional methods may well feel reluctant to revise their approach to teaching to accommodate them. Many teachers, including myself, were taught that extra-mural classes should be divided into two equal sessions, the first half being devoted to a lecture and the second to discussion. As young students used to attending lectures in the daytime can rarely concentrate for more than half an hour, it hardly seems realistic to expect adults who have already had a full and busy day to attend a continuous lecture lasting from forty-five minutes to an hour. In practice I have always found that a mixture of lecture and discussion has been much better than a rigid division into two periods, and no doubt many other teachers will have arrived at the same conclusion. Perhaps, leading on from this, it would be helpful to describe in more detail the undergraduate course, 'The Psychology of Learning', referred to in the previous chapter. It may be remembered that in that course I tried to apply the principles of programmed learning to the whole year's work, in a somewhat belated attempt to practise what I preached.

As mentioned in the last chapter (page 147), the students were given an initial test to find out how much they knew already about the concepts to be covered by the course. The following week they were given an exercise which was prepared partly to throw further light on their relevant knowledge and partly in keeping with the suggestion that one should proceed from the known to the unknown. As will be seen, the exercise was concerned with 'student learning', which was very relevant to their contemporary life in the university, as well as to the particular course of study.

Name... Date.....................

This is an exercise in concentration. Instead of allowing your mind to wander along a string of *associations*, taking you further and further away from the original *stimulus*, you are asked to look at the *stimulus* in the middle of the ellipse below and to write the first *association* that comes to your mind along the line on the extreme left (1), and then immediately look back at the *stimulus* words again and write down the next *association* that they suggest to you on the next line to the right (2). Continue this process until you have written down 20 *associations*, all to the same *stimulus*. As soon as you are sure what you have to do, concentrate on the *stimulus* words below and carry out the procedure just described.

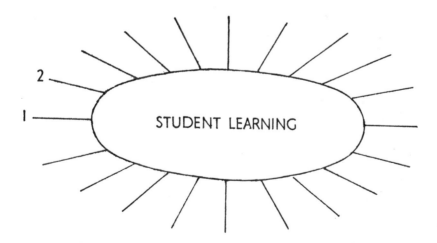

The results of this exercise were very much in line with the previous one in which the students were asked to identify concepts in the psychology of learning. Some associations were common, but after the first two or three responses they were more individual. In a group of 31 students, the most popular association was 'lectures' (made by 25 students) followed by 'books' (22), 'essay' (19) and 'library' (15). A number of words were supplied by three students, a larger number by two, but by far the largest group by only one student. On the average, each student produced five associations not mentioned by any other student. The whole exercise was helpful both to the student and the teacher, and produced a great deal of useful material.

This particular exercise has various uses, apart from the one mentioned here. Any concept can be placed in the ellipse and, when carried out on the chalkboard with a group, this procedure is useful at the beginning of a single lecture or a course of lectures in breaking the ice and getting the students involved in the topic concerned. An instance was cited at the beginning of the last chapter where the members of the audience were asked to provide their associations to the concept of programmed learning before hearing a talk on this subject.

Another use of the repeated association technique is in terms of the enrichment of concepts, which was given as the aim of learning and teaching in the last chapter. It is useful to compare the student's associations to a concept at the beginning of a course with those that he makes at the end. Most people have a general idea about the meaning of a concept, but the better a person understands it the richer is its connotation to him. For instance, most people know what is meant by an 'average' or 'mean', and could readily work out a football team's goal average by adding the goals it had scored and dividing by the number of matches played. Without a course in statistics, however, they might not be aware of the difference between arithmetic means, geometric means, and harmonic means. Nor might they be aware of the mathematical definition of an arithmetic mean as that value in a frequency distribution from which the algebraic sum of the deviations equals zero. Similarly, they might not be aware of the place of the arithmetic mean in a moment's system, where it is seen as a fulcrum and related to measures of variance, skewness, and kurtosis.

Following the exercise calling for associations to the concept of student learning, the students were given information about criterion behaviour, as described in the last chapter. The next exercise asked each student to consider the aims of a university education in general and his own degree course in particular in terms of criterion behaviour. With these goals in mind, he was then asked to rank university learning and teaching techniques in the order in which they contributed to the criteria. The methods and rankings are shown in Table 1, together with the mean rank for each method for the 31 students involved. Again, a wide range of individual preferences is shown, although there seems to be a fair amount of agreement about the unhelpfulness of lectures and examinations.

Table 1

RANKINGS OF UNIVERSITY TEACHING METHODS ACCORDING TO THEIR RELATIVE CONTRIBUTIONS TO THE REQUIREMENTS OF AN UNDERGRADUATE DEGREE

Rank	Books	Projects	Tutorials	Seminars	Informal Discussions	Essays	Practicals	Lectures	Exams
1	9	6	5	2	4	2	3	1	0
2	2	5	7	5	5	4	4	0	0
3	6	7	3	3	4	5	3	1	1
4	5	2	5	5	5	3	3	2	0
5	4	5	4	4	2	4	4	3	1
6	2	3	0	5	2	6	6	2	5
7	2	1	6	3	1	6	7	3	1
8	1	2	0	2	5	1	1	14	4
9	0	0	1	1	3	0	0	5	19
Mean	3.4	3.6	3.8	4.6	4.6	4.6	4.7	7.0	8.0

In the early stages of the course, the results of the exercises were discussed with the whole class. Later, however, each student was allowed to proceed at his own pace, and was given a new exercise as soon as the previous one had been satisfactorily completed. Perhaps an extract from one of these later exercises will serve to show how an attempt was made to apply the principles of programmed learning in a very general sense to the whole of a course.

Name.. Date...........................

Read the attached extract from Tolman's article 'Operational Behaviorism and Current Trends in Psychology.' Review Mednick, Ch 2 (especially pp. 18-20). Review Hill, Ch 1.

A *general definition* of a concept gives an abstract and broad description of the meaning of that concept (connotation) and is the kind found in *A Dictionary of Psychology* by James Drever.

An *operational definition* of a concept specifies the concrete operations whereby the concept can be observed (denotation) and measured, and is the kind used in actual experiments and research.

A. For each of the statements given below indicate whether it is a *general* or an *operational* definition, and then supply the alternative. (Any reference material may be consulted).

    Example
    (i) *Latent learning* is a type of learning which is not evident in performance at the time when the learning is taking place. (*General* definition).

    (ii) *Operational* definition: Rats deprived of food for 22 hours do not make less errors in a six-unit alley T-maze after several daily trials without food at the end of the maze. Their error curve drops acutely the day after food is first introduced into the goal box, showing that *latent learning* had taken place in the previous trials. (H. C. Blodgett, 1929).

1. (i) *Anxiety* is a chronic complex emotional state with apprehension or dread as its most prominent component. (...........................definition).
    (ii) ....definition:

2. (i) *Experimental neurosis* occurred when Pavlov trained dogs to discriminate between a circle and an ellipse, and then progressively altered the shape of the ellipse until it became more and more like a circle. When the ratio of the horizontal to the vertical diameters reached 9:8 the dogs became extremely disturbed and disorganised. (...........................definition).
    (ii) ....definition:

3. (i) *Knowledge of results* is the knowledge which an individual or group receives relating to the outcome of a response or group of responses. (..............definition).
    (ii) ....definition:

B. Provide both a *general definition* and an *operational definition* for the following concepts:
    1. *Delayed Reaction*
    2. *Reinforcement.*

It will be noticed that the exercise is coupled with required reading, and this does seem to ensure that students read the necessary material when it is most relevant. By combining reading with an exercise, the teacher knows that the student has both read and understood the set books as he goes through the course. Exercises can be combined with tutorials and, as not all students reach the same stage at the same time, the teacher is able to devote his attention to small groups, the members of which are roughly comparable in their knowledge of the subject.

In this course, branching was used for enrichment rather than for remedial purposes. Thus the best students were able to study each topic in greater depth than those who took longer to grasp the main concepts. An interesting finding from this mode of procedure, where the students were allowed to proceed at their own pace, was that those who assimilated the material most quickly were the ones who tended to be regarded as problem students by other lecturers. It would appear that their restlessness in lectures was due more to boredom and eagerness to get on than to bad manners or discourtesy. Suppressing bright students is just as harmful as coercing dull ones—neither approach produces the best results from the individual student's point of view.

So much for the application of the principles of programmed learning to a whole course. Now let us look at the use of published programmes and the more formal approach to programming.

An example was given in the last chapter of how specially-prepared programmed material helped adults to operate electric sewing-machines. The principles of programmed learning seem so obviously relevant to the teaching of such practical skills that it is surprising to find that there are really very few programmes available in this area. On the other hand, many programmes have been published relating to liberal studies, where teachers may not so readily expect to find them. A full list of programmes available in book form, or for use in conjunction with a teaching machine, is provided in the excellent *Yearbook* edited by Cavanagh and Jones. This book can be recommended not only for its well-indexed catalogue of programmes in print, but also for the various articles concerned with all aspects of educational technology. Practising teachers will find much here that will be helpful to them, and theirs will be an unusual subject if they cannot find at least one programme relating to it. The following are just a few of the topics on which programmes have been prepared and published: carpentry, civic affairs, English literature, French literature, history, logic, music, photography, and religious education. For each programme listed, full information is given as to the publisher, the price, the age group for which the programme is intended, whether it is in book form or for machines, whether it is linear or branching, the number of frames it contains, and the rough amount of time taken to complete it. Broadly speaking, linear programmes are better either for young people or for older people tackling new and difficult subjects. Branching programmes contain more information on each frame and are better suited to students and older people. Before recommending a programme, however, a teacher would be well advised to try it himself and to assess its usefulness in terms of the aims of his course and the backgrounds of his students. The old controversy between linear and branching programmes has now died down and it is recognised that both have their uses. Quite often a combination of the two is most appropriate. Stones' text, referred to in the last chapter, is a good example of a programme which draws freely from both approaches.

Many programmes are available in book form and are relatively cheap to buy. Films are usually more expensive and there is the additional price of the machine required to present them. These tend to be mostly of the branching variety and may cost over £200. Much simpler machines, costing only a few pounds, can be bought for presenting linear programmes, which are either published on rolls of paper or can be made up by the teacher. However, the general principles of programmed learning can be followed quite simply with home-made equipment, which need be no more elaborate than a large envelope. If about three-quarters of the opening of the envelope is cut away to a depth of about one inch on the left-hand side, a linear programme can be presented on foolscap paper by simply drawing it slowly out of the envelope. The frame is revealed in the cut-out on the left, while the answer is covered by the protruding portion of the envelope on the right. When the paper is pulled out further to reveal the next frame, the answer to the previous one also comes into view and the student can check his response immediately. Again, it is a question of flexibility and imagination, and no one eager to use programmed learning will find cost a deterrent.

There is no reason why teachers should not write their own programmes, tailor-made to their own specific requirements. It takes time, but the teacher usually learns a great deal in the process. The principles of programmed learning can be used as a guide, and for linear programmes the book *Programmed Learning in Perspective*, referred to in the previous chapter, provides an excellent recipe. For those wishing to try their hand at writing a branching programme, *Basically Branching*, by Rowntree, serves the same purpose.

These two chapters cannot provide more than an introduction to programmed learning, but teachers who would like to know more about the principles and practice of this approach to education can take it further by consulting the books already mentioned, and by reading the other references given in the bibliography. Richmond's *Teachers and Machines* and *Teaching Machines and Programmed Learning,* by Kay and others, give a fairly general approach to the subject, while for a more detailed account of the history and various aspects of programmed learning there are two very useful collections of articles in the books edited by Lumsdaine and Glaser, and by Smith and Moore.

For those who wish to keep abreast of the most recent advances, there is the *Journal of Programmed Learning and Educational Technology.* This was first published in 1964 and now has international status. It is the official publication of the Association for Programmed Learning, which has its headquarters in London. The Association's conference is held annually in various parts of the country and provides an opportunity for those interested in programmed learning to come together and discuss their experiences and research. The proceedings of two such conferences have been published as companion volumes with the title *Aspects of Educational Technology.*

The development of programmed learning in Britain can also be seen in the establishment of various centres specifically designated to look into its application in schools, universities and industry. The National Centre for Programmed Learning at the University of Birmingham was established in 1965 at the invitation of the Secretary of State for Education and Science. This centre collected information from all over the country and also offered training courses in programmed learning. It was mainly concerned with primary and secondary education. The Audio-Visual Aids and Programmed Learning Unit at the University of Liverpool is more concerned with the application of educational technology to higher education, including adult education, with special emphasis on programmed learning. The applications of programmed learning to training in industry are being studied by the National Industrial Programmed Instruction Centre at the University of Sheffield. These centres exist to provide information where necessary and to help those interested in using programmed learning in their own spheres of education.

One of the heartening things about educational technology is the way it spans all stages of education and training. The fundamental problems of learning and teaching are common problems, and much can be gained from co-operation between students and teachers in trying to solve them. Such co-operation, however, requires co-ordination at a national level, and it was partly to satisfy this need that the National Council for Educational Technology was set up in 1967. The Chairman of the Council is Sir Brynmor Jones, Vice-Chancellor of the University of Hull, and the Director and his staff have their offices in London. They are concerned with all aspects of educational technology as it applies to education and training in schools, colleges, industry, and in the public and armed services. The Council's latest contribution to this field is the

L

sponsorship of a new journal called *Educational Technology,* starting publication in 1970.

Programmed learning has come a long way since that pioneering article by Skinner in 1954. Its growth reflects an increasing awareness of the inadequacy of traditional methods of teaching in the world today. Knowledge and populations are expanding at an alarming rate, and some rethinking is essential if our educational system is to stand any chance of coping with the demands that will be made on it in the future. We must plan now and try out new methods before it is too late. Primary education has changed most in the last twenty years, but the pressure is gradually moving upwards and teachers in adult education would do well to prepare themselves for the changes that are bound to come. They could try applying the principles of programmed learning in their own work for a start. It should prove to be a liberating experience.

FURTHER READING

Cavanagh, P. and Jones, C. *Yearbook of Educational and Instructional Technology 1969/70 Incorporating Programmes in Print* (1969)

Dunn, W. R. and Holroyd, C. *Aspects of Educational Technology,* 2 (1969)

HM Stationery Office. *Audio-Visual Aids in Higher Scientific Education* (1965)

Jamieson, G. H. 'Age, speed and accuracy: a study in industrial retraining', *Occupational Psychology,* 40 (1966), 237-42

Kay, H., Dodd, B. and Sime, M. *Teaching Machines and Programmed Learning* (1968)

Kelly, T. *Adult Education at the Crossroads,* Inaugural Lecture, University of Liverpool (1969)

Leytham, G. W. H. 'The universities' need of audio-visual aids and programmed learning', *New University,* 3 no 1 (1969)

Lumsdaine, A. A. and Glaser, R. *Teaching Machines and Programmed Learning* (Washington 1960)

McLeish, J. *The Lecture Method* (Cambridge 1968)

Mager, R. F. *Preparing Instructional Objectives* (Palo Alto, California 1962)

Maslow, A. H. 'Goals of humanistic education', *Esalen Papers* (1968)

Richmond, W. K. *Teachers and Machines* (1965)

Rodger, A. 'Symposium on the selection of pupils for different types of secondary school.—VIII. An industrial psychologist's point of view', *British Journal of Educational Psychology,* 19 (1949), 154-9

Rowntree, D. *Basically Branching* (1966)

Skinner, B. F. 'The science of learning and the art of teaching', *Harvard Educational Review,* 24 (1954), 86-97

Smith, W. I. and Moore, J. W. *Programmed Learning: Theory and Research* (Princeton 1962)

Stones, E. *Learning and Teaching: A Programmed Introduction* (1968)
Thomas, C. A., Davies, I. K., Openshaw, D. and Bird, J. B. *Programmed Learning in Perspective* (1963)
Unwin, D. and Leedham, J. *Aspects of Educational Technology* (1967)

13 The Uses of Broadcast Material

E. G. Wedell

Since this book is intended to provide a practical text for the teacher of adults, this chapter does not explore all the highways and byways of the educational uses of the broadcasting media. It concentrates rather on a discussion of the ways and means in which adult educators may best benefit from the general open-circuit broadcasting services. The use of the *technical installations* of radio and television for closed-circuit transmission is discussed in Chapter 10.

WHAT ARE ADULT EDUCATORS OFFERED?

There is little doubt that in recent years the quantity of adult education programmes offered by British broadcasters has tended to outstrip the use made of them by potential clients. The difficulty of relating supply precisely to demand is one of the besetting problems of the broadcasters. This difficulty is compounded in the case of adult education programmes by the comparatively small size of the audience in broadcasting terms. The conventional devices for measuring broadcasting audiences reckon to deal in millions rather than hundreds of thousands. Adult education audiences tend to fall into the latter range. Thus the audience-research methods which provide useful data for much of the general programme area are not capable of yielding much useful information about the audiences with which adult educators are concerned. The statement in the first sentence of this paragraph can therefore be no more than a generalisation.

The facts are that the two British Broadcasting Corporation television channels at present provide about $7\frac{1}{2}$ hours a week of adult education programmes, and the commercial channels, under the Independent Television Authority, provide (depending on the region) between 2 and 5 hours a week on its single channel. This total output of 10-12 hours a week consists of 15-20 different programme series on a wide range of subjects. Some series are repeated in the course of the week so as to allow people to see it who were unable to view the first transmission.

On the BBC sound services adult education is transmitted on Radio Three for 5 hours a week, a total of 10 programmes of which 3 are repeated on Radio Four on Saturday mornings.

THE EDUCATIONAL ROLE OF BROADCASTING

In view of the inadequacy of the general arrangements for audience research, attempts are continually being made by the broadcasters to identify the users of this substantial output. Education, it must be remembered, is not part of their output on sufferance; it is part and parcel of the statutory responsibilities of the broadcasting organisations, which are to provide broadcasting services of education, information and entertainment.[1]

Indeed the educational function of broadcasting is deeply ingrained in the history of British broadcasting which makes fascinating reading. The story of the BBC's pioneering work in this field is told in detail in the second volume of Professor Briggs' *History of Broadcasting in the United Kingdom*.[2] The difficulty throughout has been caused by the reluctance of the broadcasters to draw a sharp dividing line between the three elements of broadcasting. This has stemmed from a sound educational instinct, but has made for a good deal of trouble over the years in the way of demarcation disputes. The arguments have been healthy in that they have always kept at the forefront of the broadcasters' attention their inescapable responsibility to make value judgements as part of their programme decisions; value judgements about their audience—its willingness and ability to consider new ideas and its readiness to exert itself in assimilating difficult material.

There have recently been signs that this traditional dilemma is becoming too irksome for the broadcasters and that they are trying, as inconspicuously as possible, to evade it by formalising and categorising both their audiences and their output. It has to be faced, they argue, that some people like *only* pop and some people *only* classical music. Why then should they not be provided with what they like and *only* with that? When this argument is applied across the intellectual and cultural board it leads to a compartmentalisation which is disastrous to the integration of the whole personality with which adult educators are concerned.

These questions of broader policy are essential to the dicussion of the uses of broadcast material for adult education because they affect the output, quantitatively and qualitatively. They inevitably condition the general level of interest and trouble which the broadcasters take over this sector of their responsibilities.

TYPES OF ADULT EDUCATION PROGRAMME

Programmes forming part of the adult education output can be classified in a number of ways. The most obvious distinction, which also denotes the main difference between the output for schools and for adults, is that between courses designed for institutional or group viewing and listening and those for viewers and listeners at home. A different type of distinction may be made between programmes related to an externally devised syllabus, such as a General Certificate of Education course, and courses whose contents are determined by the broadcasters and their advisers. Again, it is possible to make a rough and ready distinction between liberal and vocational courses; between courses designed for a particular interest group and those addressed to the general audience.

This wide range of programme types makes it difficult for the broadcasters to identify their objectives in general terms. Their vision tends to be further obscured by the need to keep in touch with many different agencies in adult education. A look at the composition of the advisory committees of the BBC and the Independent Television Authority suffices to indicate the range of interests seeking to influence the character of the output; interests which not infrequently clash. The post-school output of the BBC is supervised by the Further Education Advisory Council which includes representatives of the Committee of Vice-Chancellors and Principals, of the Association of Teachers in Colleges and Departments of Education, the National Advisory Council on Education for Industry and Commerce and the National Union of Students, as well as of bodies more immediately concerned with adult education. The ITA's Adult Education Advisory Committee is somewhat less broadly composed, although a number of the institutional representatives are members of both bodies. Both, as their names indicate, are purely advisory and, unlike the School Broadcasting Council, have no executive responsibility.

The BBC radio output is contained mainly in Radio Three, which has its Study Hour between 6.30 and 7.30 from Mondays to Fridays. Three of the ten programmes transmitted during this time are repeated on Radio Four between 10.30 and 12 on Saturday mornings. There are also some programmes, intended particularly for women, on three weekday early afternoons in the autumn and winter. The main weekday timing of the radio programmes is such that it is not impossible for organised groups to listen to them together. It is less certain that the time is suitable for adults at home who wish to listen to them on their own. The competition of the evening meal, of children seeking help with their homework, or merely of the early evening television programmes, may well be too much for all but the most determined listeners. This difficulty is borne out by the audience figures. The BBC estimate that Radio Three attracts 2 per cent of the total radio audience, compared with 46 for Radio One, 34 for Radio Two and 18 for Radio Four.[3]

The radio series are intended to help the listener to:

> acquire a body of knowledge (such as of war and its effects on the present 'age of conflict'), achieve an improved skill (such as spoken mastery of a foreign language), or receive a sequence of specific impressions (perhaps of Renaissance literature) or insights (into problems of modern industrial management, for example). Whatever the subject matter, it is presumed—and experience bears this out—that many listeners, motivated by the broadcasts, will want to pursue the topic still further on their own, with the help of reading lists, records, study notes etc that are often available in support.[4]

Choice of subjects presents something of a problem. Which are suitable for television and which for radio? In the event the choices are not always the most logical. A series marking the tercentenary of the death of Rembrandt should really be on television. Since this could apparently not be achieved, it was decided to transmit it on radio and to accompany the radio series with radiovision, thus making available a selection of colour slides and study notes to support the broadcasts. A series on music might well be at the other end of the continuum from a series with a visual theme, and therefore likely to be best transmitted on the radio. But even these judgements cannot be made with certainty except in the context of each individual series. There is, moreover, a large middle ground where either sound or sound and vision can usefully be employed. The teaching of languages and of the types of subject which, on television, tend to be treated mainly by 'talking faces', can often be as effective on sound radio as on television. The adult educator has to face the fact that there is a fair amount of competition both between the radio and television sides of the Further Education Department at the BBC and between the BBC and the ITA. This gives rise to a good many diseconomies if one applies the criterion of coherent planning. At the same time competition spurs on the respective production units and certainly makes for greater effort.

The BBC television output in further education currently falls roughly into two halves; the vocational and the liberal. There has recently been considerable emphasis on management and related studies. A three-pronged experiment in 1968 was concerned to use both radio and tele-vision to provide material for students taking the Ordinary National Certificate and diploma courses in business studies. 'There were three principal tasks—first, to provide an introductory series on English law; second, to provide a dramatised case study of the management account-ancy of a small business; and third, to provide a background series on radio, introducing applied economics as a background to the firm in the television case study'.[5] Another important area of vocational study to which the BBC has contributed is education. The series *Teaching Adults* and *Mainly for Teachers* have tried to make effective use of television for the in-service training of teachers. The third main area in the vocational field is that devoted to technical education and training.

The use of all these series by organised groups has been largely dependent on the timing of the transmissions. The series for technical colleges was in fact transmitted in one of the school slots around mid-day. The teachers' series was given its first showing on a Sunday morn-ing, with a repeat at 4.10 pm on Mondays, in the hope that teachers might view it after the end of the school day. The adult education series was shown on Sunday mornings with a repeat transmission on Saturday mornings. This, unexpectedly, appeared to be quite popular.

The Independent Television output, as has already been indicated, tends to be more exclusively concerned with liberal and leisure time pur-suits, at least as far as the network programmes are concerned. Most of the more vocational series, such as *Postgraduate Medicine, Farm Progress, Mathematics in Primary Schools,* are produced by the regional companies in response to needs and interests expressed in their respec-tive regions. Although the output here is more haphazard, it may well be that the use made of regional series is proportionately much greater than that made of national series, since the lines of communication between broadcaster and adult educator are so much shorter and regional series often derive from some clearly expressed need. It is ironic that this responsiveness to regionally expressed needs tends to be greater the smaller the area concerned. The west of England, the Border country and north-east Scotland are examples of areas which appear to derive a good deal of benefit from the close co-operation between educators and broadcasters.

THE INTEGRATION OF BROADCASTING WITH OTHER MEDIA

Much of the opposition to the use of broadcasting for educational purposes derives from the argument that education is essentially a matter of encounter between teacher and taught, of personal confrontation, of the give and take of argument and of the dynamics of the learning group. One of the challenges that broadcasting has had to face from its early days is that it is essentially a one-way medium and that it is therefore educationally at best of little value, at worst positively harmful in encouraging too receptive and uncritical an attitude on the part of the student.

There has also been criticism on grounds of the ephemeral character of the media. Programmes are gone as soon as they are transmitted; there is no means of recapitulating or going back over an argument. It is sometimes forgotten that the same tends to be the case in the formal lecture. Unless there is time for questions, elucidation and even interruption, there is little to choose between it and the evanescent television or radio programme.

Thus the broadcasters and educators have long been concerned to develop ways and means of reinforcing the broadcast impression and of securing feedback from their audiences. Reinforcement has been developed in a variety of ways.

Support Literature

The earliest and most important was the production of support literature for educational series. The roles of such literature vary. In some cases it is merely an edited script of the series itself. This, of course, does no more than retain in print the spoken words of the programme. In television, where the point of using the medium is, or should be, the optimal use of the visual characteristics of the medium, the publication of the script is rarely adequate since the text covers only a part of the information given by the complete programme.

A second type of support material is the textbook written to accompany a series. Each chapter may deal in general terms with one of the programmes in the series to which it relates. But the book does not repeat the material contained in the programme. Rather it expands, elucidates and underpins the programme, preferably leading the student on to attempt to answer questions arising from it, to develop the argument in his own way and to follow leads given in it in some form of experimental activity, practical work or observation. This is one of the most difficult types of support literature to produce; only occasionally does one see examples of it.

A third type of support literature takes the form of teachers' notes. Where a series is intended mainly for group viewing, it is valuable for the teachers to have an idea of the thread of the argument, of the main points to look out for, and of the best way of using what may be only

18 to 25 minutes of programme in a 90- or 120-minute session.

The means of distribution of support material varies. The BBC has its own publications department which handles large quantities of printed material on both educational and other subjects. The department is efficient and experienced. Few of its publications can, however, be obtained other than by post from its headquarters. But experience has confirmed the obvious, namely that literature which is easily available from bookstalls and newsagents reaches a much wider public than material for which one has to make the effort to buy and send a postal order.

Both because they do not have elaborate publications departments, and in order to achieve wider distribution, the Independent Television companies tend to make arrangements with paperback publishers for the handling of their support literature. Where this has been done and literature has been freely available from bookstalls etc, the results have sometimes been spectacular; 50,000 or more copies of a text have been sold compared with 3,000 or so in the case of literature available from the television company concerned. But on occasion publication also involves adjustment of the material so as to make it usable outside the context of the television series to which it relates. This may weaken its contribution to the effectiveness of the integrated teaching package.

The Use of Kits

A second means of involving the broadcast audience more effectively is the distribution of kits containing material for experimental or practical work arising from a broadcast series. This type of activity is suitable only for some subjects, such as the sciences, possibly mathematics, possibly some arts and crafts, etc. Moreover, kits tend to be expensive to produce and to distribute. Thus the method has not been developed very far as yet. The most notable example of the use of an experiments kit was the joint ABC Television and National Extension College series *First Steps in Physics*. Here a kit cost 59s 6d (£2.97½) and was bought by just under 4,000 people. In the view of the *Times Educational Supplement* at the time:

> This kit at first appears an ill-assorted collection of oddments, but a closer examination reveals that it is exceptionally well-planned, serving a wide variety of illustrative experiments . . . It is possible to mention several aspects of a school physics course which must be absent from a course of home study. But having recognised these inevitable limitations, it is necessary to praise this kit as a well thought out and reliable guide for those lacking personal tuition in a well-equipped laboratory.[6]

This quotation indicates the limitation of this kind of support material. Clearly a series of this kind is much more effective if it can be related to some type of face-to-face tuition.

Face-to-Face Tuition

Increasingly, therefore, those responsible for adult education programmes on radio and television strive to provide at least some opportunities for personal encounter between their viewers or listeners and some competent teachers in the subject concerned. At this point organised adult education provision plays a vital part. The problems are obvious, and a good deal depends on the structure of the particular situation. If the programme series is made available to a class formed for the purpose the problem of arranging face-to-face tuition does not arise, although other problems may. One of these is timing. The programmes may not be transmitted on a day and at a time when all members of a group can attend. At present the only television programmes transmitted at reasonable times for group viewing outside the home are those shown on BBC 2 at 7 pm on weekdays. It is usually desirable for a group to meet some time before the beginning of the transmission, so that the teacher or leader may establish the link with the previous meeting and there is some leeway for latecomers and for any preparatory work intended to make the broadcast material more assimilable. Thus for a 7 pm programme a group should be timed to begin at 6.45 pm.

It appears that the agreement made between the Open University and the BBC provides for the use of the time between 5.30 and 7.30 on BBC 2 on weekday evenings and for certain daytime periods at weekends for Open University courses.[7] This means that these periods will, from 1971, no longer be available for general adult education transmissions. It is doubtful whether suitable alternative times can be made available for them. Accordingly the outlook for adult education programmes on television outside the degree course programme of the Open University is uncertain.

Where group viewing at a convenient transmission time is impossible, group use can none the less be made of such material as long as the members of the groups are willing and able to view or hear the programmes at home. In some ways such use may well have a reinforcing effect, since a weekly cycle of programmes related to a weekly cycle of course meetings will help to maintain interest and act as an incentive. It is, of course, essential that the teacher should have seen the programme, so that he may be in a position to clear up misunderstandings arising from the students' unfamiliarity with the subject. Even so, disputes will arise about the understanding or interpretation of particular sections of a programme. In such cases the broadcasters will usually be in a position to provide a script of the transmission to the teacher concerned.

The possibility of integrating broadcast material with the work of adult education classes depends on many factors. A useful account of the efforts made in relation to the BBC 2 television series *The Social Workers,* transmitted from October 1965 to February 1966, sets out some of the difficulties encountered.[8] Of the 280 groups which started viewing the series 230 were thought to have completed it. And although a good deal of benefit was derived from the corporate activity, this also disclosed some incidental disadvantages. There was some tendency to regard the role of the group as being to criticise the production of the programme rather than to learn about social work. It is likely that this side effect derived from the novelty of the situation for many students and from the close concern of the broadcasters to obtain feedback from their audience. A less predictable side effect of an adult education programme was recorded by Dr Belson in relation to a French language series *Bon Voyage* transmitted by the BBC in 1953. Here it was found that 'the programme had produced an increase in viewers' knowledge of the words and phrases, and of the facts presented, but that this was accompanied by an increase in viewers' apprehensions about language difficulties and about visiting France generally'.[9]

Residential Courses

Where regular group work in connection with a series cannot be arranged, either because not enough people in a particular locality are interested or because weekly meetings are not convenient, short-period residential courses may be of value. It has taken some years for both the broadcasters and the short-term residential colleges to appreciate the potential for co-operation in this field, but this is now beginning. Again there are difficulties, some of which were experienced in relation to the *First Steps in Physics* series transmitted by ABC Television in 1966-67. As Professor Lipson, the director of one of the courses held in connection with this series, has pointed out, the people attending 'had taken the course for a remarkable variety of reasons. Some wanted to top up the physics that they were already doing; some wanted to understand the application of physics to ordinary phenomena, not having done any physics at all before. The one common quality was keenness . . .'[10] The broad span of background knowledge of students drawn together for a short period without an element of selection tends to limit effective learning at short courses. Thus it is best to hold courses related to broadcast adult education series towards the end of these, thereby giving the participants the maximum amount of common background knowledge. The reinforcing role of the residential session is, of course, also important. It must not take place at a point in the course at which the majority of students have given up!

THE RELATIONS BETWEEN BROADCASTERS AND ADULT EDUCATORS

The effective use of broadcast material for adult education depends on close co-operation between those producing the material and those using it or helping others to use it. Essentially the difficulties encountered in developing such co-operation fall into two groups: differences between the broadcasters' scale of operation and that of the local adult education organisation; and differences in the time needed for the planning and execution of broadcast material and the time scale on which local adult education tends to operate.

As Richmond Postgate, the BBC's Controller of Educational Broadcasting, has pointed out, 'In all broacasting, a regard for numbers is plainly necessary, since communication to a greater number of people simultaneously is its essence'.[11] He qualifies this for educational programmes. 'The numerical canon of success in Further Education broadcasting is . . . the proportion of the chosen target that is achieved, rather than the total audience',[12] but the chosen target must be reasonably large if open-circuit transmissions are to be justified. Some broadcasters argue that, because this is so, there is little justification for the use of the general services for lengthy and detailed educational series. These, so the argument goes, attract audiences which, in broadcasting terms, are tiny and contract to even smaller numbers by the time they end. Thus they take up a disproportionate amount of air space which could be more usefully employed for shorter courses opening up areas of study which viewers and listeners could then follow up through their local further and adult education agencies.

There is a good deal of sense in this argument, and although it is likely that the Open University courses will run counter to it the development of other adult education broadcasting may well be in this direction. If this were to be accompanied by a less hesitant attitude on the part of the broadcasters to the direct linking and cross-promotion of their activities and those of the adult educators, the pattern of provision might well be better than it is at present. Adult educators should, in any case, never hesitate to press the broadcasters to make better use of their media to publicise available provision in local areas. This is at present easier in Independent Television by reason of the division of the national network into regional transmission areas which are smaller than those of the BBC. The development of area television by the BBC should improve the position in this respect.

The problem of feedback continues to exercise broadcasters. The advisory councils and committees already mentioned are intended to ensure this at national level. Like other bodies of this kind, these committees tend to respond to initiatives taken by the broadcasters rather than playing a dynamic role of their own. Their main practical task is to recommend approval of adult education series submitted to them by the broadcasters[13].

In order to be effective, feedback must be related to a particular series and must be speedy and representative. Efforts have been made from time to time to build specific arrangements for feedback into a series itself. These arrangements usually founder on the rock of the time factor. The turn-round of information from broadcast series to viewer, back to the broadcaster, and into a later programme, tends to take not less than a fortnight. Programme series are usually written as a whole and tend to be recorded on videotape well before transmission, partly to ensure that mistakes can be rectified and partly to make economic use of production and studio facilities. Thus both editorial and technical difficulties stand in the way of the amendment of a series. The best that can usually be done is to build into it from its inception one or more revision programmes, leaving these to be transmitted live or to be recorded a day or two before transmission on the basis of reports and questions submitted by viewers. The possibility of leaving a short period for live material at the end of a recorded programme has also been explored, but I do not know of a series in which it has been successfully employed.

Viewers' and listeners' correspondence can, of course, be dealt with outside the programme. If this is encouraged and reaches substantial proportions, however, it makes additional demands on the subject specialists, and these they may not always be in a position to meet.

Other ways of linking adult educators and broadcasters have been tried over the years. The BBC's further education liaison officers act as the Corporation's eyes and ears and do excellent work. The education officers of the Independent Television companies tend to work individually and have to deal with the output both for schools and for adults. On the other hand, the regional television companies tend to maintain advisory bodies of their own which bring them into close and regular touch with educational interests in their areas:

Meetings with teachers planning to use a given course have also been arranged from time to time. These can be very helpful in giving the users advance information about the handling of a subject, about likely problems and about any feedback arrangements that have been made.

They also establish personal contact and help to create a sense of partnership between broadcasters and adult educators.

THE EVALUATION OF BROADCAST MATERIAL

If adult educators are both to influence and to make effective use of broadcast material, they need to know how to evaluate it. They must be aware of what the media can and cannot do, they must have some familiarity with what goes on in a television or radio studio, and they must establish criteria of their own which will help them in the assessment of what they and their students hear and see.

It is difficult to generalise about the potential of the media. Clearly, at present, any teaching which relies on the sense of smell cannot be undertaken either by radio or television. Until colour television became available the same applied to teaching for which discrimination between different colours is essential.

But although broadcasting restricts the range of teaching in some respects it extends the range in others. For instance, a recorded television experiment in science can telescope the actual time taken to complete it and enable something to be demonstrated on the screen which would not fit into the compass of a normal face-to-face lesson.

Familiarity with a television or sound studio is important, and all adult educators interested in working with broadcast material should seek to spend some time in one. Usually this can be done by arrangement with the education officer of the broadcasting organisation concerned.

The establishment of criteria of judgement is largely a personal matter and I can do no more here than to suggest some headings.[14]

Assuming the basic purpose of an adult education series to be to help viewers and listeners towards progressive mastery or understanding of some skill or body of knowledge, it is possible to arrange the criteria for evaluation in six groups.

Content
   Does the material cover the appropriate area of knowledge?
   Is the content academically reliable?
   Is the material developed consistently?
   Does the broadcast teacher master his subject?

Teaching Method
   Is the objective of the course clearly defined?
   Is each step oriented firmly towards this objective?

Is there adequate linkage forward to future programmes and back to previous programmes?

Does each programme achieve internal coherence?

Learning Aids

Does the series reflect an understanding of the pschology of adult learning?

Are there adequate pauses for reflection on the part of the student?

Are appropriate gaps provided for exercises or repetition by the student?

Are the materials to be used for practical work (if any) easily accessible to the student?

Is the programme constructed so as to provide the right mixture of tension and release?

Does the programme allow for variation in the level of concentration?

Is the pace appropriate to the subject and the length of the programme?

Student Participation

Has the character of the target audience been clearly identified, in particular in its educational level(s) and its mastery of technical terms?

Does the programme encourage as much student participation as the subject will allow?

Is the length of the programme appropriate to the absorptive ability of the audience?

Use of the Medium

Are the resources of the medium (sound or sound and vision) fully exploited?

Has the right decision been made about the role of the broadcast teacher?

(ie Should he be an expert in the subject with no media experience?

Should he be a good broadcaster with little knowledge of the subject?

Is one teacher adequate?

Does the series need an identified 'face' at all, or would 'voice over' be more appropriate to the material?)

Are the visuals, captions and animation adequate?

Are the visual and aural elements well related?

Is the camera work adequate?

(ie Are there adequate establishing shots? Enough close-ups?)

Is sufficient time allowed for the audience to take in the visual content?

Production

Does the production cover the subject area as fully and exhaustively as the objective of the series requires?

Does the direction suggest that the director understands the educational purpose at each point?

Do the individual programmes hang together? Is there a sense of unity?

Does the series help the conscientious viewer towards progressive mastery or understanding of its subject?

Clearly not *all* criteria apply to *all* adult education series, and aspects not listed here may be relevant. Anyone using broadcast material regularly will be able to build up his own check list and develop ways of using it effectively. In ideal circumstances teachers should have an opportunity of previewing a whole series, but this is not often likely to be possible. Thus much of the critique is bound to be retrospective. It is important that teachers should not let this inhibit them from submitting their evaluations to the broadcasters. Only in this way can each side make the most of the knowledge and experience of the other.

THE USE OF GENERAL PROGRAMMES

There is no doubt that in terms of the general level of knowledge and understanding of the world more is learned from the general programme output than from the specifically educational output of the mass media. It is essential, therefore, for adult educators to take a lively interest in the standard of the general programmes, to develop criteria of judgement, and to encourage this among their students. Often a general programme or programme series can be used effectively for the teaching of adults, especially in the fields of literature, politics, the social sciences or the appreciation of music or the arts. The problems of timing which are so acute in much adult education programming may well not apply to general programmes, making it easier for students to see or hear them within or outside the context of a teaching situation. As and when the types of technique currently available for the recording and replay of sound radio material are more generally available to television audiences (ie video-recording and replay facilities at reasonable prices), adult educators will not suffer from the inconvenient times of the programmes made available for adult education. They will be able to record

M

transmissions by time switch at any time of the day or night and replay them for themselves and their students whenever and wherever is most convenient. The relationship of the adult educators to the broadcasters will have come of age.

NOTES

1　Television Act (1964), Section 1(4)(a) and BBC Charter
2　Briggs, A. *History of Broadcasting in the United Kingdom,* Part II (Oxford 1965), 185, 226
3　BBC. *Record 66* (1969), 4
4　BBC. *Yearbook* (1969), 81
5　BBC. *Yearbook* (1969), 78-9
6　Quoted in Wedell, E. G. and Perraton, H. D. *Teaching at a Distance* (1968), 17
7　HM Stationery Office. *The Open University* (1969), 21
8　Hancock, A. and Robinson, J. *Television and Social Work* (1966), 15-16
9　Belson, W. A. 'Learning and Attitude Changes Resulting from Viewing a Television Series *Bon Voyage'*, *British Journal of Educational Psychology,* 26 part 1 (1956)
10　Wedell and Perraton. *Teaching at a Distance,* 18
11　Quoted by Groombridge, B. in Moir, G. (ed). *Teaching and Television* (Oxford 1967), 93
12　Ibid
13　For a fuller discussion of the role of advisory bodies in broadcasting see Wedell, E. G. *Broadcasting and Public Policy* (1968) 213-33
14　Here I lean heavily on a useful check list for the members of the jury for the Adolf Grimme Prize for Adult Education Programmes in West Germany.

FURTHER READING

Barrington, H. 'A Survey of Instructional Television Researches', *Educational Research,* 7 no 1 (1965)
Belson, W. A. *Effects of Television on the Interests and Initiatives of Adult Viewers in Greater London* (1959)
Cassirer, H. R. *Television Teaching To-day* (Paris 1960)
Charnley, A. (ed). *Face of the Earth: Teaching O Level Geography by TV and Correspondence* (1969)
Current Developments in Educational Television (New York 1962)
Davis, D. *The Grammar of Television Production* (1960)
ITA. *Educational Television, Some Suggestions for a Fourth Service* (1963)
BBC. *Educational Television and Radio in Britain* (1966)
Educational Television: The Next Ten Years (Washington 1965)
Greene, Sir H. *The BBC and Adult Education* (1961)
Groombridge B. (ed). *Adult Education and Television, a Comparative Study* (London and Paris 1966)

Groombridge, B. 'Adult Education—the Formative Phase', in Moir, G. *Teaching and Television* (Oxford 1967)

Hancock, A. and Robinson, J. *Television and Social Work* (1966)

Hickel, R. *Modern Language Teaching by Television* (Strasbourg 1965)

Maclean, R. *Television in Education* (1968)

Perraton, H. D. 'Eleven Broadcasting Experiments', *Home Study* (Cambridge 1968)

Schramm, W., Lyle, J. and Pool, I. de S. *The People Look at Educational Television* (Stanford 1963)

Scupham, J. *Broadcasting and the Community* (1967) (Ch 7 on Educational Broadcasting)

Scupham, J. 'The Control and Conduct of Educational Broadcasting', in *Sociology of the Mass Media Communicators, Monographs of the Sociological Review* (Keele 1969)

Ford Foundation. *Teaching by Television* (New York 1961)

HM Stationery Office. *The Open University* (1969)

Third EBU International Conference on Educational Radio and Television (Paris 1968)

Waller, J. and Gross, R. *Learning by Television* (New York 1966)

Wedell, E. G. *The Use of Television in Education* (1963)

Wedell, E. G. and Perraton, H. D. *Teaching at a Distance* (1968)

Wedell, E. G. *Broadcasting and Public Policy* (1968) (Ch 5 on the relationship between the broadcasters and their audiences)

Wiltshire, H. and Bayliss, F. *Teaching Through Television* (1965)

14 Tuition By Correspondence

Walter James

Tuition by correspondence is both a specific mode of adult education and a technique used in many forms of adult education which would not be considered mainly as correspondence. It is also itself increasingly incorporating techniques and modes of instruction used in other forms of adult education. If the focus is on the word *tuition,* then tuition by correspondence could be said to take place any time anyone receives a book by post; but if we focus attention on the idea of *learning* by correspondence, then its distinguishing feature is that the essential interaction between student and tutor is by correspondence—a route to learning which uses the pen and the typewriter rather than the voice as its vehicle.

It has been estimated, though not with any degree of precision, that it is a mode of education engaged in at this time by half a million people in Britain and nearly three million in the United States.[1] MacKenzie's recognition, while making a study of correspondence instruction in the United States for the Carnegie Corporation, that 'for way too long, this important segment of the educational system in the United States had been neglected—and even ignored—by the academic community, by researchers, and by authors who explore the various functions of education'[2] would be true for Britain, where the first major study of correspondence instruction has only recently been published.[3] Childs claimed towards the beginning of the 60s that 'we badly need research on the methodology of teaching by correspondence. Practically no research has been carried on in this important area',[4] and he was able to repeat towards the end of the decade[5] an assertion made in the middle of it that 'it is probably safe to say that if one were to make a list of the areas of notable achievement in the correspondence study field, research would not head the list.[6] By far the greater part of the volume of writings on correspondence education are descriptions which range in reliability from the persuasively promotional to the more objective apologias. If one were to exclude information presented by those who

180

have a vested interest and a product to sell, there would be relatively little left.

It is being increasingly recognised that the two explosions—of population and of knowledge with its associated technological developments—are producing a situation where more people need to be educated more frequently; and the traditional modes of adult education, which were more adequate when stability was a greater characteristic of life than it is now, are increasingly coming under strain or can only remain satisfied with their contribution so long as they ignore the changing situation. For the responsive but hard-pressed adult educator who wants to reach more people, reach them for more things and reach them more opportunely, correspondence instruction confers advantages which may well provide him with some of the opportunities he is seeking.

The major advantage of education by correspondence is that it frees the educational institution from what Wedemeyer has called 'learning chained to teaching in space and time'.[7] Traditional adult education, which has not slipped these chains, has restricted itself to an audience which finds it convenient and desirable to be in the places made available at the time specified. Perhaps it could obtain a new audience, or not tax so much the audience which it has, if it did not demand their attendance at all, or did not demand it so frequently. About half the correspondence-course students surveyed in the Manchester project (E. G. Wedell, R. Glatter and S. Subramanian, 'Study by Correspondence', Dept. of Adult Education, University of Manchester (1969) rated as important reasons for choosing a correspondence course, first, that going to classes would be uneconomical of time for them, and second, that the time available for them to study varied at different periods of the year.[8] Countries like Canada, Australia and New Zealand, with sparsely settled and inaccessible regions—with 'nine hundred and ninety nine square miles and seventy-nine pupils'—have been forced to recognise correspondence education either as a full substitute or as a supplement to other educational facilities.[9] It is perhaps too easily assumed that in highly populated islands such as Britain there is no 'outback' problem—but it needs to be asked whether the failure to provide certain kinds of adult education facilities in remote rural areas does not itself contribute to the depopulation of those areas.

Inaccessibility is, however, but one side of the coin, whose other face is inconvenience. Wedell and his colleagues in their survey of correspondence course students found that 'nearly 50 per cent of the students live in conurbations having a population of 700,000 or more; about 10 per cent in "minor conurbations" with a population between 250,000 and 700,000'[10]—a finding which is not so 'unexpected' as they found it, if the experience of countries such as Denmark, Sweden and

Holland, which have highly developed correspondence education facilities operating in educationally well-endowed urban environments is borne in mind. In town as well as country there are likely to be students to reach.

To reach out to the individual student who is isolated or wants to isolate himself confers advantages through creating imperatives for the teacher. Perhaps there is an element of exaggeration in the claim that 'the correspondence school pupil . . . is a human individual, not merely a unit of a flock moving or stopping just as the drovers and dogs direct',[11] but the contrast does indicate one of the characteristics of correspondence education which it may be difficult to achieve in some classrooms. The answer to the question posed originally in 1930, 'in what classroom, under our present educational condition, do 40 or more contacts take place between teacher and student in one course?[12] would still, I suspect, disquiet those who see frequency of such contact as being a major contribution to learning. It is still probably true of correspondence courses now, as it was in 1962, that 'the typical syllabus is a rather rigid instrument. It tends to carry all students through the same set of experiences irrespective of previous experiences or capacity to learn'.[13] But it is also true that correspondence tuition has the capacity to provide for adjustment to individual differences, since each student can proceed at the rate and with the materials most appropriate to his needs.

'The question of cost' is obviously, as Holmberg claims,[14] 'a practical snag' for the non-profit-making—and non-subsidised—correspondence college which may want to integrate the new media and new methods into correspondence study, and for the commercial college which 'must finance its own operations and meet its stockholders every year' the cost of securing the individualised instruction made possible by programmed courses is likely to be prohibitive. Paddon claimed in 1965 that 'it is obviously going to be extremely difficult, if not impossible, for commercial colleges to have very many programmed courses within the next, shall we say, ten years'[15] and subsequent events do not appear to have proved him wrong. Paddon went on to suggest a reduction of the economic barriers by asking whether it would be feasible and acceptable to set up in Europe, and perhaps in America, a system of mutual exchange, so that courses which were costly to produce were made more widely available. The Carnegie study, four years later, added a pessimistic postscript to this line of thought, for it seemed to MacKenzie and his colleagues 'that one of the most striking weaknesses we encountered was the almost complete lack of supplier co-operation', and he noted, for example, that in spite of the scarcity of resources, particularly at the university levels in the 9,000 courses offered by universities and colleges in the United States there was 'a great duplication of effort'[16] If correspondence education is to be used more widely by British adult educators they would do well to avoid the practice of their American precursors in this field. High initial costs for some modes of correspondence instruction need not be a deterrent to course production as long as the freedom to reach large audiences which worldwide methods of communication and distribution give is not restricted by a parochial attitude among educational administrators.

Nevertheless, in spite of the cost of producing some modes of correspondence instruction, there is evidence to suggest that, taken overall, it is a highly economic means of education. Many of the developing countries such as Malaysia, Rhodesia, Venezuela, India, Algeria, Ethiopia, Thailand, Indonesia, Zambia, Malawi have increasingly sought, through an extending use of correspondence education, to reconcile their high educational aspirations and needs with their small educational manpower and their inadequate economic base for educational activities of the more traditional kind. Since there are no countries which cannot be described as developing, and few, if any, which do not have to reconcile the first of these characteristics with the other two, the extension of correspondence education could well be a more economic way of providing education for the many than merely multiplying the traditional facilities would be. The most significant economy is achieved by the separation of teaching and learning that exists in correspondence education, for this enables the gifted teacher to be more widely available. The newer methods and materials being increasingly used in correspondence education extend the possibilities in this direction. Programmed instruction, audio tapes, radio and television (whether on open or closed circuits), not only make the teacher available at a distance but extend the ways in which he is available. Even where developed educational institutions exist there is little doubt that correspondence education of this kind would be an effective supplement and extension of their activities. It is at least open to question whether a small force of adult educators is best employed in face-to-face situations. Could it not be that a small and élite band of full-time teachers would be more profitably employed producing, in a correspondence course framework, instructional materials whose use could be exploited by the larger numbers of part-time teachers? Certainly the two full-time extra-mural tutors who produced the Nottingham University correspondence course *The Standard of Living* reached more students through only a one-shot exercise than they would have reached in ten years of more traditional teaching.

Even if the adult educator is not to act wholly or mainly, but only partly in this way, there are some modes of behaviour which he will have to eschew, as well as some which he will have to cultivate. The last state of the art will be worse than the first if he follows the sequence which one prominent American adult educator claims as characteristic of the preparation of American university transatlantic offerings:

> 1. Ask a Prof or a Department for a course. 2. Take the outline as received (and give thanks if it shows a bit of commendable originality—curses if it is a mess). 3. Set it up in lessons as per usual—with bits of information we need to add. 4. Arrange for references, library use and a *bit* of promotion. 5. Print it on hectograph, mimeograph or more recently off-set press. 6. Send it out a few lessons at a time or more recently, under one cover—sedately conservative![17]

The adult educator seeking to extend himself as a teacher through correspondence education is more likely to succeed if he follows the three-stage process which Flanagan suggests as appropriate for all modes of education which have the concern of the learner at heart:

> The formulation of detailed educational objectives in terms of behaviour changes anticipated; a set of procedures for measuring or assessing the performance of the student in terms of the specific knowledge, ability, skill or attitude defined in the objective; and the identification, selection and organising of the instructional methods and materials in terms of manageable segments called teaching-learning units.[18]

To perform this threefold task poses special difficulties for the correspondence educator.

With regard to the first stage, the adult educator is often loath to formulate detailed educational objectives, for this seems to him to go against the spirit of liberal education. It is also open to question whether, even if he overcame his scruples and formulated such objectives, he could express them in terms of the behaviour changes anticipated. As a correspondence educator he will have a further problem; he has to get the student to accept the course objectives for himself and to assess his own readiness before attempting to reach them. The stimuli which motivate adults to learn are increasingly well known; the means by which these stimuli are presented in instructional materials are still largely at the trial and error stage. When to these problems is added the necessity for some students and the usefulness for others to be compensated for the loneliness which correspondence education can often demand, the problems are formidable. The solutions most often attempted are the attractive presentation of instructional material, the personalisation of the relationship between the teacher and the taught, the provision of counselling facilities, and arrangements for some face-to-face learning.

With regard to the second stage, the designing of assessment procedures which not only accurately measure the degree to which objectives
have been attained but which are also helpful to the student, still has
to be achieved in many educational situations. In correspondence education the programming in of feedback and assessment opportunities is
vital, for the isolated student is denied the immediate feedback from the
teacher and his fellow-students that the classroom situation provides.
In correspondence education the teacher will find additional difficulties,
for there is a sharp break in the learning-feedback cycle and much of
the feedback is presented non-aurally. Attempts to solve or to reduce the
effect of these problems usually require clarity in expression so that
misunderstandings are reduced; an increase in the number of responses
which can be auto-checked; and the development of non-written communication (eg the telephone and the audiotape) between teacher and
student.

With regard to the third stage, the adult educator has not been the
most notable in harnessing the range of methods and materials to his
purpose. In many classrooms 'chalk and talk' is the major operational
mode, and where it is not this is often only because the chalk is left idle.
The adult educator will have to open himself out to the possibilities
which educational technology makes available.

It is, however, when thinking of this third stage in the process that
one begins to wonder whether thinking of it within the context of
correspondence education is not unnecessarily limiting. To subordinate
the variety of instructional technologies and methods exclusively to the
requirements of correspondence education is to restrict them somewhat
unnecessarily. The educational development of the student is best served
by other than adherence to a single and exclusive mode of educational
operation. The development of a systems approach to educational tasks
in which, first, the appropriateness of learning activities, media equipment, and material to meet particular learning objectives is determined
and, secondly, the selected items are arranged into a sequence which
maximises student progress, is increasingly seen as more relevant than
the insistence upon the supremacy of a particular mode for all the
objectives of any particular course. The Articulated Instructional Media
Project at the University of Wisconsin, the Extension Course Institute's
auto-instructional programme developed by the United States Air Force,
and the Program for Afloat College Education adopted by the US Navy
are the outstanding examples of an approach which, though it is being
increasingly adopted for technical education in Britain, has as yet made
little impact on the provision of social and humanities studies for adults.

Perhaps the traditional British adult educator is alienated from
correspondence education because it is concerned with the vocationally-

motivated and not the students for whom learning is sufficient reward; it produces courses which are particular and narrow, not broad; and it is wedded to specific and unmodifiable objectives, not general aims which are modified by the particular students the course has enrolled.

Adult education will be the poorer if this condition remains. Though the provision of adult education is increasing, there is no evidence that it is increasing proportionately to the increase in demand or in need. It seems economically unlikely that there will be an adequate extension of the existing modes of operation. Correspondence tuition—the reaching of the many by the few—avoids the necessity for an uneconomic form of the extension of extension. There are few sectors of adult education that would not benefit from its use; but in university extramural education in particular it might enable the recovery of a lost purpose; the taking of the university to those who would not or could not come to it.

NOTES

1   Wedell, E. G., Glatter, R. and Subramanian, S. *Study by Correspondence* (Manchester 1969)
2   MacKenzie, O. 'The Status of Correspondence Instruction in the USA', a paper delivered to the 8th International Conference of the International Conference on Correspondence Education (Paris 1969), 2
3   Wedell, Glatter and Subramanian. *Study by Correspondence*
4   Childs, G. B. 'Problems of Teaching by Correspondence Study', in *Report of the Conference on Newer Media in Correspondence Study* (Austin, Texas, 1962)
5   Childs, G. B. 'Recent Research Developments in Correspondence Instruction', paper delivered to the 8th International Conference of the ICCE (Paris 1969), 1
6   Ibid
7   Wedemeyer, C. A. 'The New Educational Technology', *Journal of the American Dietetic Association,* 53 no 4 (1968)
8   Wedell, Glatter and Subramanian. *Study by Correspondence,* p 76
9   Haight, R. C. 'Nine Hundred and Ninety-Nine Square Miles & Seventy-Nine', *Phi Delta Kappa,* 19 no 8 (1937)
10 Wedell, Glatter and Subramanian. *Study by Correspondence,* p 81
11 Broady, K. O. 'What the Correspondence Method Can and Does Contribute Towards Meeting the Modern Demands Made on Education', *Proceedings of the 5th International Conference of the ICCE* (Banff 1957), 37
12 Bond, O. F. 'Foreign Language Instruction by Correspondence', *National University Extension Association Proceedings,* 13 (1930)
13 Childs. 'Recent Research Developments . . .'
14 Holmberg, B. *Proceedings of the 7th International Conference of the ICCE,* 43

15 Paddon, T. W. *Proceedings of the 7th International Conference of the ICCE,* p. 54
16 MacKenzie, O. 'The Status of Correspondence Instruction in the USA,' 4. See also MacKenzie, O., Christensen, E. L., and Rigby, P. H. *Correspondence Instruction in the United States* (New York 1962)
17 Davies, J. L. 'Graphics and Manipulated Media', in *Report of the Conference on Newer Media in Correspondence Study* (1962), 47
18 Flanagan, J. C. 'Functional Education for the Seventies', *Phi Delta Kappa,* 49 (1967), 1

15 A Rationale For Adult Education

H. A. Jones

Education, even in closed societies like ancient China or feudal Europe, has always been a gateway to privilege. When privilege came to be something to feel ashamed of (roughly since 1789) education also became involved with ideas of equality. In Britain adult education in particular has seemed obliged to justify itself by its role on the large stage of the world rather than in the mind and sensibility of the recipient. In finding a rationale for what we do now in our adult classes, a good guide may be to look first at this traditional view of the purpose of adult education before asking in what ways it has lately been modified and to what extent it will continue to serve the needs of a very different society.

Briefly the tradition rests on the assumption that in a democratic society responsibility is spread equally to all men and it is therefore essential that all men shall be prepared for it. Hence those who have enjoyed the benefits of education have a duty to share it with those who have not. A concern for the under-privileged, not merely to repair their lot but to enable them to take their place as full and responsible members of society, has been present in most of the movements in British adult education.

The earliest formal moves were concerned mainly with men's spiritual health. They derived from a pious awareness that the lower orders were cut off from the Word of God by their inability to read. The eighteenth-century Circulating Schools in Wales, that took a massive step towards universal literacy, set out to teach people to read the Bible, the Book of Common Prayer and the Catechism; and the Adult Schools started in Nottingham in 1798 had a similar aim of educating people for salvation.

These movements were not the result of popular demand; the people to whom they were addressed may have lived in a condition of misery and ignorance, but there is no evidence that they felt themselves spiritually deprived. Yet the response shows that a genuine if inarticulate need had been touched. Some of the most notable, as well as the earliest achievements in British adult education occurred among the poor and the submerged, who would now be thought the most unresponsive. Needs and demands are not the same and adult educators may have become too concerned with demand.

When, however, in the nineteenth century, men became aware that they were politically under-privileged, the needs that adult education came to serve were more directly felt. Those who provided education for the poor were often inspired as much by political apprehension as by true philanthropy. 'We have a deep interest in their morals', wrote the founders of one educational society early in the century. 'As in every country they are numerous, it involves our personal security.' Such candour was unusual, but the fear that the tide of radical ideas might rise to a revolutionary flood was never far from the minds of many of the men who laboured to establish educational opportunities for the poor. All the same, it would be unjust to diminish the role of genuine philanthropy in the foundation of the Working Men's Colleges (as expressed, for instance, by F. D. Maurice in 1855), or of many of the Mechanics' Institutes and other forms of adult education in Victorian England.

Similarly among the working classes themselves, the need for political and economic power as a way of escape from intolerable conditions of life was equated with educational opportunity, and all the radical movements of the century had an educational wing. Every Co-operative Society still has its education committee.

In all these movements education is viewed as a means to some other end, religious at first, social and political later. The mere continuation of elementary schooling, though this often did take place in adult life, was not part of the purpose; nor was the completion of technical and vocational training. The distinction between liberal and vocational education was already established.

The man who, more than any other, summed up this tradition and handed it on to the present century was Albert Mansbridge, who founded the Workers' Educational Association in 1903 to bring the teaching resources of the universities into the movement for universal adult education. He had already seen what the university extension movement had done during the previous thirty years to spread university teaching up and down the country and to contribute especially to the higher education of women; but his concern now was with the working people. In his thought there are four main elements. First, education is a right that all should enjoy whatever their previous attainments or capacities. As he wrote in *An Adventure in Working Class Education,*

> The educational system of this country has always tended to set a premium upon cleverness. That premium must be removed and set upon devotion rather than upon achievement. The forbidding ideas connected with the word school and education . . . have to be removed, and the shyness of people who have little knowledge, or who think themselves not clever, overcome.

But secondly, for all men, including working men, education is also a need.

> A man who throughout life will work with his hands needs general education for the same reason that it is needed by a specialist like a lawyer, or a doctor, in order that he may be a good citizen . . . As a member of a self-governing nation he must acquire the civic qualities which enable him to co-operate with his fellows, and to judge wisely on matters which concern not only himself, but the whole country to which he belongs.

The words come from *Oxford and Working Class Education,* the report of a great conference held at Oxford in 1907 at which Mansbridge and his Workers' Educational Association persuaded the University to set up a formal machinery for university teaching to working people. The university tutorial class has been an important form of adult education ever since.

Thirdly, adult education is 'for life not livelihood'. Technical and vocational studies, important enough in themselves, belong to a pre-adult stage of life. They ensure the economic conditions in which living can begin, but it is with the next stage, the quality of life itself, that adult education is properly concerned.

Fourthly, the adult's experience of life fits him for making judgements about what is relevant to his educational needs. Mansbridge wrote

> The time has gone by when any one section of the people can do things for any other section without their co-operation. The magnificent prospectuses presented to the public by capable educational administrators have had no magnetism in them, because they have been created apart from those for whom they were designed . . . Adult students will not take lectures passively like undergraduates; they desire to diagnose, to criticise, or to add to the views taken up by any teacher. They are ready to give their experience, their cherished ideas, to be reconsidered in the light of fuller knowledge.

These concepts are enshrined in the famous *1919 Report,* a survey by a government committee in which the whole range of adult education, including the work of the local education authorities, is brought into a single view and proffered as a prime contribution to the creation of that land fit for heroes that was expected after World War I. The Report itself is a noble and cogent plea,

> that adult education must not be regarded as a luxury for a few exceptional persons here and there, nor as a thing which concerns only a short span of early manhood, but that adult education is a permanent national necessity, an inseparable aspect of citizenship, and therefore should be both universal and lifelong.

Again there is this emphasis on education for democratic responsibility. 'There is latent in the mass of our people a capacity . . . to rise to the conception of great issues'. What they need is 'the development of an open habit of mind, clear-sighted and truth-loving, proof against sophisms, shibboleths, clap-trap phrases and cant'. Adult education is the means of developing it.

How firmly these aspirations took root can best be seen, not from the large claims of organisers and theorists, but from the words of students themselves. In *Learn and Live* W. E. Williams and A. E. Heath published the findings of an enquiry amongst adult students of the day. Time and again the motive that comes up is what the authors call 'through-self-for-society'. Here are a few examples, taken at random, of students' statements of the purpose of adult education as they had experienced it:

> The development of individual personality—and then the development of the ideal of service to the community.
>
> To create or foster a vision of social responsibility.
>
> To liberate the sympathies, develop the intelligence, and to unfold the natural capacity of the individual, so as to fit him to . . . make his contribution to the life of the society.

(There is, of course, much more than this in *Learn and Live*; accounts of intense personal discoveries made through study, or equally intense disappointments, of estrangements from family or friends through the acquisition of new interests and values; and also the ventilation of ancient prejudices that have remained quite untouched by the best efforts of devoted teachers. The whole book is an unrivalled insight into the complexities of adult students' reactions.)

One other element in the tradition remains to be mentioned. It has been contributed by another voluntary body, the Educational Centres Association, and is usually called the 'centre idea'. This stresses the importance of self-government in adult education. If part of the object is to help people to understand and carry out their responsibilities to the community, it may best be achieved by creating a small community of all the students in a given place and entrusting the planning and management to them. The centre is thus more than a collection of classes under one roof. It is a laboratory for experiments in democratic co-operation and action.

What I have been trying to sketch here is the classic British tradition of adult education. It is concerned with the quality of life of all ranks of men, but especially the under-privileged. The aim is the enlargement of knowledge, not simply for its own delight or for personal enrichment or advancement, but for the discharge of democratic responsibility; the values derive from the fact that in a democracy no man is an island, that the quality of our communal actions depends on the quality of the individuals' values by which they are decided. As a rationale for adult education in a disordered and changing world the relevance of this tradition is evident enough.

It is therefore odd that Britain is almost the only part of the world in which such a purpose for adult education has been formulated. In Asia, Africa and Latin America there are very large schemes of adult education that know nothing of democratic responsibility; they are concerned simply to teach people to read, write and count, to improve their tillage and husbandry, and to induce them to practise elementary hygiene. Yet, successful as these schemes have been, they cannot keep pace with the growth of population. The number of literate people grows but the number of illiterates grows faster; this task of fundamental adult education does not work itself out, it gets bigger. At the other extreme, in North America, technological and industrial developments have brought vast and ever-changing demands for qualifications, and a great deal of adult education is directed to satisfying them. In short, over the greater part of the world, much of what goes on in the name of adult education would be hardly recognisable as such to most British adult educators, in the light of their own traditions.

But those traditions have been changing radically of recent years too. The voluntary agencies—the universities (or some of them), the Workers' Educational Association, the Educational Centres Association—energetically carry on their traditional tasks in the traditional way, but they have added many new forms to them. Especially, under the influence of ideas and knowledge from abroad, the old distinction between vocational and non-vocational education has been questioned and some people would now distinguish between 'adult education' (in the traditional framework) and 'the education of adults', which is much wider and includes all forms of education—technical, professional, liberal or recreational—that adults may follow. The term 'continuing education' has been borrowed from America and is sometimes used to denote the kind of work which, though liberal in manner and often directed to the traditional social purposes, takes the student's job as the starting-point. Examples would be day-release courses in industrial relations, some forms of management studies and certain postgraduate studies in science and technology. A whole new area in the education of adults has been opened up by the need to retrain people for new jobs as technological change destroys their old ones, and the evidence is mounting that this can be done more effectively when the context and the reason for change are understood. 'Industrial training' is too narrow a term for the opportunities that the Industrial Training Act has created. And finally, the concept of 'permanent education', which has become current in Western Europe, is finding its way into discussions of adult education in Britain. This is a term that I shall return to later.

The tradition also comes under question in a quite different way. The most spectacular increase in adult education in this century has not been in any of the old forms. It has been in the evening institutes, where adults in their hundreds of thousands are to be found in a range of classes that again have little to do with citizenship and democratic responsibility. Indeed many of the activities have never previously been contemplated as part of an educational curriculum: antiques, for example, or soft furnishing, flower arrangement, car maintenance, boat-building, bridge and golf. No one planned this growth. Religious zeal, philanthropy, social reform have no part in it. It simply represents popular demand on a scale never known before. What are we to make of it all? Do we sweep it aside as trivial, a play-school for the toys of affluence? Do we accept that the customer is always right, and, if this is what the customer wants, should it not be provided? Do we call it adult education and include it as part of that adult education that the *1919 Report* described as 'a permanent national necessity'? If so, on what terms? It seems to lead straight back to what is meant by adult education.

A few years ago E. M. Hutchinson, Secretary of the National Institute of Adult Education, examined this problem of definition in a paper in the UNESCO journal *Fundamental and Adult Education* and suggested the following: 'Organised opportunities for men and women to enlarge and interpret their own living experience'. It will be seen that there are three main elements in this formula. First, it differentiates between organised activities and the informal educative effects of television, the press, contacts with other people at work and play, or what the French call cultural diffusion. So there is a difference between a golf class and a game of golf. Secondly, it stresses the element of active participation, to enlarge the experience. Thirdly, it involves interpretation. There is nothing here about citizenship and social purpose, but I believe that, if the practice of adult education is examined in the light of Hutchinson's

N

definition, the relevance of the traditional rationale to this whole new area of work becomes clear.

I find it helpful (though I know it is now somewhat unfashionable) to revert to the old word 'liberal' to describe the features of adult education that are in question here. Nowadays the word is often taken as meaning little more than 'non-vocational', but historically it has a more precise and more apt meaning. It is derived from the Latin *liber*, meaning a free man, and in classical times a liberal education was the education of the free citizen as opposed to the slave. The domain of the free man was decision; he should be competent to judge any issue, social, political, religious, military, moral, and his education prepared him to do so. Hence, of course, in the intervening centuries the ideas of liberal culture and a liberal education have become associated with the training of a ruling élite, and this is one of the reasons why they arouse suspicion now. If, however, the word 'liberal' is taken in its original meaning, reinforced by other associations—humanity, reform, generosity—it may serve as a description of the kind of adult education needed today.

There are no slaves now, but it seems to me that the pressures of our society are enslaving rather than liberating pressures, and one of the reasons for the recent spread of adult education in the particular form it has taken has lain in men's desire to ease these pressures. The submergence of small communities in the sprawl of towns, the submergence of meaningful work in the hug of vast organisations, the submergence of individual choice in the devices of mass consumption have threatened the foundations upon which men rested their sense of identity. It is not surprising, therefore, that they have turned inwards for reassurance, re-establishing their small community in the family group, finding meaningful work and a restoration of individual choice in making and doing about the family home. A number of studies, for instance by Groombridge and Robinson, have shown how widespread is this domestic culture, and it is clearly reflected in the subjects that attract the largest number to adult classes.

This picture of cosy domesticity is an incomplete one, however. For one thing, a rising divorce rate seems to indicate that home is not always a place of reassurance. Outside the ranks of the domesticated there are deserts of loneliness and alienation among the young, the unmarried, the handicapped and the old. And even where the family unit is reassuringly established and its members find support and creative outlets in working within it, it may represent its own form of enslavement, an arrested development through the enchantment of small things. Guy Hunter, from his experience of residential education, offers a perspective upon this.

There is a rough sequence in a working life which the intellectual is too apt to forget. After the first period of school and pure technical training, the worker, for the ten years from 15 to 25, is pitchforked into practical life—finding and holding a job after marriage and founding a home on small resources—while the intellectual is training himself in handling words and conceptions. It may well be that somewhere between 25 and 35, as the worker approaches a more responsible job, education should broaden his ideas of the nature of authority and responsibility, of the social and human implications of any new job, of the deeper purposes of society. Once this broadening process has been started, it may well lead on into history, literature and art. If we take the concept of 'the standard of living' it means at 21 bread and butter and the wage packet. At 30 it may include ideas of status, leisure, civic responsibility ; and at 40 and thereafter it may deepen into a concept of the good life.

Neither the path nor the pace of this progress will be uniform for all; but it is good to be reminded that, given the right conditions, horizons will continually widen as experience grows.

In other words, it is necessary to conceive of adult education as life-long, not just in the sense of being available to people of all ages, but as capable of assisting in a development that goes on throughout life.

It is true that the distinguishing feature of adult education is that the students are adults and that this refers not to chronological age but to maturity. The experience which is to be enlarged and interpreted in an adult class is already extensive and deeply held. But the possibilities of personal identity are almost infinite; at least they are not likely to be exhausted in one span of three score and ten. (This is why the Greeks taught philosophy, or the *love* of truth, and Christ the *love* of goodness, because no man can attain truth or goodness in his lifetime.) The function of adult education is to keep open the options, to prevent the arrest of development by the pressures of society, to ensure that, whatever the stage of self-knowledge or self-fulfilment that has been reached, the way of further growth is visible.

This is the point at which to return to the European concept of permanent education, in which education is seen as one single process, extending throughout life. If this concept were put into practice it would mean that the whole of schooling was planned, not as a preparation for a job or as a self-sufficient preparation for life, but as a preparation for the whole further range of educative possibilities that would become appropriate at successive stages of adult life. It would mean that school curricula would be pruned of those things that are more appropriately treated later, and conversely that adult education could take for granted certain experiences of learning and attitudes towards it. But it does not mean, of course, that adult education must always be formal; cultural diffusion through the mass media, through amenities like libraries, theatres, sports grounds, and through varied informal agencies, is part of the total process. If there is a weakness in the formulation of this concept it is in its apparent over-emphasis on the personal development of the individual, to the exclusion of his role in society. This feature of the British tradition is still of great significance. Freedom, the goal of a liberal education, can only be exercised among one's fellows—it had no meaning for Robinson Crusoe.

If we accept this view of adult education as something which may have different goals at different stages of individual development, there are certain practical consequences. In the first place, the idea of 'subjects' as the proper stuff of education may have to be modified and the students' declared interest allowed to be the starting point, even if this is simply to make a dress or a cake or to maintain a car. The proposed activity will be scrutinised with three questions in mind. Is this something that can be learnt effectively (ie with a perception of excellence in its performance) in the kind of situation we can provide? Is it something in which questions of value and judgement will properly arise? Is it something that will afford insights into the human relationships of those involved? If these tests are satisfied there is, at least potentially, an acceptable educative situation and the question becomes one of method by which the activity can be pursued in this liberal way.

(This is easily said. It would be foolish to underestimate the demand thus laid on the teacher of, say, flower arrangement or car maintenance, art history or elementary Spanish. The teacher needs exceptional ability, but one of the tasks of adult education is to make its participants exceptional, and training the teachers is an inescapable part of adult education.)

Conversely, we have also to recognise that, for the attainment of these liberal goals, some kinds of activity are more promising than others: those, for instance, where the sensibility is deeply engaged, as in the appreciation of the arts or in the most openly creative work in writing, music or the visual and plastic arts, or where hard thought is needed, as in philosophy, history, science and the social studies. Whatever the student's starting point, these are the directions in which he should be led, simply because they are avenues with longer vistas.

Thirdly, we have to recognise that adult education will not be a simple or tidy activity. We are teaching people, not subjects, and shall have to operate on a number of levels according to the maturity and previous knowledge of the individual student. I am not here thinking of the problem of mixed abilities in the same class, for that may offer an opportunity as well as a problem: the insights and skills of the more able students can help the rest because they enlarge the pool of experience and judgement available to the whole group. I am thinking of Mansbridge's stress on devotion rather than cleverness.

At the outset of a class the syllabus and scheme of work will be dictated by the needs of the specific group of students. These lie in the past, embedded in the matrix of reasons that have brought the students there. Throughout the course, however, the teacher's eye will be fixed on the future, the next plateau of learning towards which each student will be climbing, for it is the climb that matters and not the altitude reached. In one of the creative arts, like painting for example, the teacher will start with the assumption that none of the students *is* an artist (in the sense of one who will produce works of lasting merit), but the whole purpose will be to ensure that each student learns to see as an artist sees, recognising in his visual experience the obligation to establish priorities and choose which bits will go into his picture and which will be discarded. If he cannot then realise his vision in paint, for all his striving and all the help of the teacher, no matter; he will have discovered what it feels like to be an artist—his world will be the bigger. Or in a language class the aim will not be precision in translation or grammatical accuracy (like the ancient classics master who is reputed to have said 'This morning, boys, we begin reading the *Agememnon* of Aeschylus, a veritable treasure-house of grammatical irregularity'); it will rather be the imaginative enlargement that comes from grappling with a world whose features and experiences are to be handled with French or German or Russian words rather than English—the discovery of what it feels like to be a Frenchman or a German or a Russian. And in philosophy one learns, not just to repeat what philosophers have said, but to think in the way that philosophers think.

I am not here denying that adult students should seek high standards of performance or knowledge, or that they often attain them, but merely emphasising that the educative element lies in the process by which they do so, the way in which the progress is made, in the 'devotion' of the pursuit and not in the thing produced.

Fourthly, keeping open the options may well stir up at any stage of life a return to the quest for qualifications. The second start of the mother with the grown family, the retraining of men whose jobs have been superseded, the progress of the late developer towards academic achievement, the attempt to qualify for a career that in youth had seemed hopelessly out of reach—all these are beyond the normal scope of non-vocational adult education. Yet they are means of liberation, a genuine way of approach to the good life, for which the techniques of adult education are entirely appropriate.

Finally, whatever the formal context, whether in responsible body classes or evening institutes, industrial training centres or colleges of further education, an essential part of adult education lies in the forming of active relationships within the group. These will be of different kinds. The teacher meets the student in his role as student, and the teacher's authority within the subject gives guide-lines for their interaction; they are both, as it were, wearing uniform and know where they stand. But the students meet one another just as people, each bearing his personal baggage (with very indistinct labels) of experience, attitudes and prejudices. Unless they are cocooned into silence by a lecturer's monologue or by chatty patter accompanying interminable demonstrations, the members of an adult class cannot fail to interact, bringing their values, the bases of their choices and judgements, their limits of tolerance and their capacity for co-operative action into the relationships they form with one another and with the tasks of the class. Herein lies the social relevance of adult education. If this pattern of relationships also embraces other participants in a centre the social relevance is enhanced.

J. A. Simpson, HMI, has summed up this theme with the suggestion that in true adult education there will be three components: general education, aimed at sharpening the sense of identity; social education, which increases competence in meeting the demands of living among other men; and personal education, which strengthens the command of skills, bodies of knowledge or patterns of thought and feeling. Adult education conceived in this way would still be engaged in its traditional and vital task of making free men, educating the members of a free society progressively to fulfil their individuality and then to exercise it fruitfully through their interaction with their fellows; for, as Eduard C. Lindemann put it, 'we have, indeed, become weary of being counted. We want to count for something.'

REFERENCES IN THE TEXT

Maurice, F. D. *Learning and Working* (1855), Styler, W. E. (ed). (Oxford 1968)

Mansbridge, A. *An Adventure in Working Class Education* (1920), 19

Mansbridge, A. *Oxford and Working Class Education* (Oxford 1908, reprinted 1951), 51

Mansbridge, A. *University Tutorial Classes* (1913), 15

Final Report of the Ministry of Reconstruction Adult Education Committee (Cmd 321), (1919), 5. Re-issued, with a preface by Waller, R. D. as *A Design for Democracy* (1956)

Williams, W. E. and Heath, A. E. *Learn and Live* (1936), 7, 9, 10

Hutchinson, E. M. 'The Nature and Role of Adult Education', *Fundamental and Adult Education,* 10 no 3 (Paris 1958)

Groombridge, B. *Education and Retirement* (1960)

Robinson, J. 'Exploring Adult Interests', *Adult Education,* 38 no 1 (1965)

Hunter, G. *Residential Colleges* (New York 1952) quoted in Hely, A. S. M. *New Trends in Adult Education* (1962), 76

Simpson, J. A. 'Androgogy', *Adult Education,* 37 no 4 (1964)

Lindemann, E. C. *The Meaning of Adult Education* (New York 1926), 56

FURTHER READING

On all the earlier movements read Kelly, T. *A History of Adult Education,* 2nd edn (Liverpool 1970)

On the growth of the Centre Idea see Allaway, A. J. *The Educational Centres Movement* (1961)

The work of the local authorities is traced in detail in Edwards, H. J. *The Evening Institute* (1961)

A classic statement of the concept of liberal adult education is Livingstone, Sir Richard. *The Future in Education* (1941); and a helpful study of the meaning of liberal education is Jeffreys, M. V. C. *Glaucon* (1950)

Finally, on the various movements in world adult education, there is still no better outline than Hely, A. S. M. *New Trends in Adult Education* (Paris 1962)

Index